WOMEN:
BIOLOGY, CULTURE
AND LITERATURE

WOMEN:
BIOLOGY, CULTURE
AND LITERATURE

HOWARD L. SCHWARTZ, M.D.

IPBOOKS.net
International Psychoanalytic Books

International Psychoanalytic Books (IPBooks)
New York • IPBooks.net

International Psychoanalytic Books (IPBooks)
Queens, New York
Online at: www.IPBooks.net

Edited by Carol Skolnick
Cover design by Steve Powers
Book design by Dan Williams

ISBN: 978-1-949093-38-4

Printed in the United States of America

"Stories surge up out of nowhere, and if they feel compelling, you follow them. You let them unfold inside you and see where they are going to lead."

—Paul Auster

To my mother, to my granddaughter, Sabine,
And to my wife, Sue, who always has my back.

CONTENTS

MY FEET KNOW THE WAY:
A POEM FOR MY MOTHER

Today is a warm and bright Indian summer day like those that so often ease prayers for a healthy New Year, a Wednesday not unlike that Tuesday of terror and death three years ago.

There is little traffic as I exit the Lincoln Tunnel and drive east across 34th St. to the Queens Midtown Tunnel. Shouldn't I have turned north and then east through Central Park at 65th St., and then north again on Madison Ave. to 87th St., to pick up my mother for our yearly visit to Mt. Hebron Cemetery? That is where I am going this Wednesday of the year 5765, but my mother no longer lives at 110 East 87th St. She cannot greet me with a smile and a kiss, her Union Prayer Book in hand. She is buried in Mt. Hebron with my father and her parents, two of her siblings, her nephew and her sister-in-law, and my father's siblings and his mother—loved by him but not by my mother.

Our last visit to this final resting place in Queens for tens of thousands of strangers with familiar, comforting Jewish names was in 1995. The monuments of those strangers always reassured me that if they were "Devoted-Loving-Caring" husbands, wives, parents, grandparents, siblings and friends, and are to be remembered, engraved in stone, for all time that way, then so could I live to be remembered like them. In death our failings are forgiven. Their monuments give testimony to the compassion of the living.

How ironic that this Wednesday I park not ten feet from the Main St. entrance gate. That last visit with my mother, I parked a long half block away from that gate. We'd chatted, as always, on the drive across the Triboro Bridge, past La Guardia Airport and east onto the LIE for one mile until exiting at Main St. in Queens. A right turn at the first light leads to Mt. Hebron. These travel directions are not to be forgotten for they lead to treasure. That Wednesday my mother looked well, but she was not well. Why didn't I drop her off at the gate? She was not fully recovered from several recent heart attacks and was already losing vision from a growing pituitary tumor. Was I callous and inconsiderate? Or did I selfishly need her to be well and strong? She'd always loved walking, and so I let her walk. Past the gate we turned right on the first path toward the far boundary fence. She carried her prayer book in which she'd written the Hebrew names and the dates of death of those we would visit. Also written in her clutched book were the names of the living, mine and my brother's, Chaim Baer and Shmuel Avram ben David ("son of David," my father's name). Surely she never thought she'd outlive us. Perhaps we were to be with her as she walked these paths of remembrance? In her book was a time-creased map with an "x" at the block and lot of each gravesite; her treasure map.

We never looked at that map. Our feet knew the way.

That day my mother stumbled and fell. As I helped her up, I joked, "It's not your time to lie on this ground." She laughed, but maybe we both knew her remaining time on this earth was short. We would not walk together this way again.

Today I am alone as I visit my aunt Shari and her son George, my uncle Louie and his wife Gertie, my grandma Malvina—she of the white hair and beautiful hands into whose protection I ran when pursued by my at times angry mother—and her husband Morris, a grandfather I never knew. I remember and place two stones on their graves, for while alone I am not alone. My mother is with me still.

I walk more slowly to my parents' graves, aware that my walking companion could no longer walk at a march.

How strange to feel I am walking with her to visit her grave. I sit on the unadorned bench before their simple monument, both designed by my brother in minimalist style, and speak to my parents. I recite the Kaddish. I become aware that a fig tree I planted this past summer was a healing gesture of love for my father. He had planted plum, apricot and peach trees in our Grumman Avenue yard. We had longingly admired a pear tree we passed each fall as we walked familiar streets to Young Israel Synagogue for Rosh Hashanah and Yom Kippur services. I forgive myself for my impatience and anger with him. I loved him and think I have become like him. He died in 1966, and today I cried at his grave.

At the far fence, past my parents graves, lie Rose, Viola, Armin, Gizella, Pauline, Aaron, Samuel, Morris and Hanna, my fathers' siblings, in-laws and mother. My childhood lies before me, and on each monument I place two stones (except on his mother's, who was jealous and never accepted my mother).

My parents were my twin towers. They dug my foundations deep and now there is a hole in the sky above me where they once stood. I stand and they are fallen. Today Sue is buying a burial plot for us in Beth David Cemetery in Kenilworth near the graves of her parents. I will rest with her, as is right; but today I think I will miss Mt. Hebron. My feet know the way here. When I no longer walk these paths, who will visit and place stones, say Kaddish, and Remember?

As I approach the Main St. gate a middle-aged woman and her white-haired mother enter the cemetery. I nod hello; but they are talking and do not acknowledge me. They are not looking at a map. Their feet know the way.

INVERSA NORWAY SPRUCE
A POEM BY SABINE B.

In a garden he wanders
aimless.
The brush,
timid,
grazing his ankles
as sunlight seeps into his shriveled surface.

Amidst delicate flowers,
perfectly pristine,
ripe and vibrant with color,

he sees himself.
In the upward and down again sloping trunk
(a reflection of the curve of his back.
In the tenacious grip of the bark onto its skeleton
(like his skin, a mosaic of
tangled creases,
the last line of defense
before the years infect his bones
and guide them to decay).

Its limbs extend outward, yet
its fingertips barely reach
the brush it shades.

Out of touch
(just the way his trembling fingers
are unable to grasp a memory,
just the way his childhood eludes him).

Larger trees, confidently rooted,
thieves of the weeping old man's sun,
plunge him
into the damp, bitter air.

TO THE READER

This book was prompted by my near total engagement in the Dr. Christine Blasey Ford and Brett Kavanaugh testimony before the Senate Judiciary Committee, and Judge Kavanaugh's statement after the accusations against him were investigated (September—early October 2018). The timing of the hearings overlapped the 85th birthday celebrations of Ruth Bader Ginsburg who experienced bias by the legal establishment despite her outstanding scholarship and impeccable credentials, simply because she was a woman and a mother. Her persistence in the face of roadblocks led to her confirmation by an overwhelming majority of the Senate to become only the second woman Associate Justice of the Supreme Court (Sandra Day O'Connor was the first). Their stories, and the stories of women throughout history (at least some of them), provided an outlet for my frustration and became the subject matter for this book. Following Paul Auster, "Stories surge up out of nowhere, and if they feel compelling, you follow them. You let them unfold inside you and see where they are going to lead."

ACKNOWLEDGEMENTS

To Carol Skolnick, my editor, who made my manuscript better, as good as it could be. To Steve Powers, my son-in-law, who designed the cover and helped me pick an image. He is a painter and art dealer. "Woman with Roses" by Joseph Garlock (1884–1980) is in the spirit of Modernism; although the painting would seem to relegate a woman to a traditional decorative role, it is powerfully painted and I believe represents my intentions to show powerful women, like Virginia Woolf's Mrs. Ramsay and the young artist Lily who values Mrs. R.'s ability to set a beautiful table with perfect flowers, manage a houseful of guests, her own brood and her husband's neediness while retaining a capacity for empathy which Mr. Ramsay, the heroic leader of the "Light Brigade," lacks. Yes, he is physically stronger and can sail and row to the "Lighthouse," but she can feel the loneliness of the keeper and his ill son. Her symbols of power are her knitting needle and her green shawl, and to offer love on her terms. Modernism is to challenge traditional ideas of marriage, literature, culture, gender stereotypes and art. Thanks, Steve for making "Woman with Roses" available and forcing me to think more deeply about my intuitive response to a young woman caring for flowers.

My thanks to my friends and colleagues who have given of their time to read and review this book: Ute Tellini, Charles Goodstein, and, Robert Schwartz. And to the authors and artists from antiquity to the present who have provided me the privilege of living in their world and enriching mine.

WOMEN: BIOLOGY AND CULTURE: PART 1

One of the most contentious arguments in psychoanalysis has been Freud's narrow understanding of women, namely that they suffer from penis envy and that men suffer from castration anxiety which would make them into women. Many corrections, modifications and attacks on Freud as a charlatan, as well as splits into different schools of therapy, have occurred over these concepts for more than 100 years, including the total rejection of any meaningful psychology of the mind: it's all random electrical impulses, dreams have no meaning, childhood sexuality, unconscious drives and conflict theory are rubbish, we have free will, and we can choose how we live or who we live with. Well, I'm not the only one who believes this isn't so.

Let's start with biology. Embryology supports Freud's recognition of humans as bisexual, not operationally but potentially. Unfortunately, the Bible—written by men—teaches that Eve was created by God from Adam's rib, which means that God—always represented as male—made men in his image. A brief review from many sources, beginning with my Zoology Professor at Columbia (I think his name was Ryan) has established otherwise.[1]

Embryology

During the process of sex differentiation, a fetus gains characteristics of either a male or a female. Sex differentiation is initiated and controlled by gonadal steroid hormones. These hormones perform organizing functions to permanently differentiate sex organs during development. This process starts before the developing child is even old enough to be considered a fetus and is instead still an embryo. A developing human is not

---

[1] PB Press Books, OpenStax: Anatomy and Physiology. Ch. 27, The Reproductive System

considered a fetus until the ninth week of development in the uterus, whereas sex differentiation begins during the sixth week of pregnancy.

By the sixth week of development, all embryos have both Wolffian ducts and Müllerian ducts. The Wolffian ducts are embryonic structures that can form the male internal reproductive system. The Müllerian ducts are embryonic precursor structures to the female internal reproductive system. In this stage, the internal reproductive organ precursors are bipotential, meaning they have the potential to develop into both male and female sex organs given the proper chemical instructions. Hormones influence their development and each fetus will only have one of pair of these ducts by the end of differentiation.

In Males

For males, the differentiation process is started by the sex-determining region Y gene, also known as the SRY gene on the Y chromosome. This gene generates the necessary biochemistry inside of a male fetus for him to develop male sex organs. The embryonic gonads secrete a protein called the anti-Müllerian hormone, which causes the Müllerian ducts to degenerate. It also causes the Wolffian ducts to develop into the vas deferens and the seminal vesicles. The undifferentiated gonads develop into testes, and other structures such as the prostate gland and the scrotum develop.

In Females

Females have two X chromosomes, so their sexual differentiation is not signaled by the SRY gene. Instead, the absence of these cues signal their sex organs to develop. The Wolffian ducts degenerate and the Müllerian ducts persist to form the fallopian tubes, uterus, uterine cervix, and the superior portion of the vagina. The undifferentiated gonads develop into ovaries, and other structures such as the labia and vagina develop.

The embryology, accepted science, boils down to that the precursor of gender in the fetus is omni-potential but will develop as female without the male chromosome and hormone. So, which came first? Obviously, it's a moot point because both sexes are necessary for procreation. (Many would argue today that science—think of Dolly the cloned sheep—will soon change our relying on Darwinian evolution and recast how we understand—might as well say it—everything.)

Culture

Two women, Ruth Bader Ginsburg and Christine Blasey Ford, both public figures—Ginsburg an Associate Justice of the U.S. Supreme Court, and Blasey Ford, professor of psychology at Palo Alto University and a research psychologist at the Stanford University School of Medicine—have made known their life stories, albeit under extraordinarily different circumstances, to allow a snap-shot examination of the changes in attitudes toward women in America today: how far we've come and how far we have to go.

Ruth Bader Ginsburg

I like to bring the good news first, so I'll start with Justice Ginsburg's story. About the future Justice Ginsburg—to frame what I am about to write—as reported in the New York Times, January 26, 1972 (https://nyti. ms/1H98VT3):

> "In a new accelerating competition among the nation's law schools, Columbia University has just scored a major coup: its law school, to its undisguised glee, has just bid for and won a

woman for the job of full professor—the first in its 114-year history.

"The glee comes in part because the woman, Ruth Bader Ginsburg, is what the school's dean, Michael Sovern, calls 'so distinguished a scholar,' that her credentials and honors would stand out in any catalogue of professors.

"It comes too, as the University of Michigan Law School dean, Theodore St. Antoine, says, at a time when many of the country's best law schools have been 'scrambling' for women, often for the same one. Most have no women at any rung of the professorial ladder.... And the glee is likely to spread far beyond the Columbia law faculty and into the law schools, where women students have long sensed an anti-female bias.

"The appointment of Mrs. Ginsburg does not add to the handful of women now working as full professors of law, for she has been a full professor at Rutgers, the State University of New Jersey, since 1969. It does, however, mark the first time that Columbia Law has chosen a woman for a full-time post higher than lecturer, or part-time post higher than adjunct professor.... The deans say that the search for women, begun a couple of years ago but intensified considerably since then, is now under way from Harvard to Indiana University to Stanford. A major reason for this new effort, the deans said in interviews, is the increased number of women now coming out of law school, now about 10 per cent of the graduates and growing. The lack of available women in the past, they said, was the reason for the present paucity of female faculty members.

"But there were other reasons offered for the present effort too, ranging from the demand by the increasing number of female law students for female professors to an appreciation of the benefits of a diversified faculty, to the 'realization,' in Mr. St. Antoine's words, that 'law is a profession that a woman can handle as well as a man'....

"Said Professor Ginsburg, the 38-year-old wife of a successful tax lawyer and mother of a girl, 16, and a boy, 6: 'The only confining thing for me is time. I'm not going to curtail my activities in any way to please them.'....

"At any rate, her new role is far from what was expected of her in her girlhood, when, she recalled: 'No one ever expected me to go to law school. I was supposed to be a high school teacher, or how else could I earn living.'"

Justice Ginsburg has been a leader on the Court for progressive causes, including antidiscrimination cases in support of women's rights (women of all stations in life "including maids in hotels)". She has been a voice of moderation: better to go more slowly than Roe v. Wade, step by step, not an imposition on all states at once. She was famous for being close personal friends with originalist Justice Antonin Scalia, bonding over their common love of opera. She has been a model for genuine collegiality with colleagues who did not share her views; a voice for dissenting opinions.

Since her appointment to the Court by Bill Clinton (1993) and confirmed by a 96–3 vote, Justice Ginsburg has been joined by Sonia Sotomayor (2009) and Elena Kagan (2010), both appointed by President Barack Obama. When in a recent interview by Poppy Harlow, a journalist and Columbia 2005 graduate, she was questioned (as she often is) when there will be enough female justices on the court, Justice Ginsburg replied with a laugh, "When there are nine, of course."

At age 86 as of this writing, Justice Ginsburg is the oldest member of the Court and is aiming to work until 90. She's a popular icon: the Notorious RBG. Her beloved husband Marty died in 2010. Ruth credits him for supporting her every step of the way, through raising two children (and as a gourmet cook, no less) and her two cancers (colorectal and ten years later, pancreatic). Her devoted trainer watches over her 20 push-ups and 30 planks, plus weight workouts daily. Her daughter Jane Carol Ginsburg (b. 1955) is the Morton L. Janklow Professor of Literary and Artistic Property Law at Columbia Law School. (Mother and daughter are the only two full-tenured professors the law school has ever had).

One can only imagine how RBG balanced the responsibilities of law school and motherhood in the 1950s, along with the obstacle of being one of the few women then attending Harvard Law School. The challenges of a first-time mom, sleepless nights that interfered with her daunting study schedule would be enough to make any woman and most men buckle. (An aside: As an intern working every-other night shifts, I would share the night-time feeding schedule with my exhausted wife by cradling our infant son in a rocking chair, a sweet time as I nursed him with her breast milk and struggled to stay awake and not to let him slip from my arms.) But her determination to succeed and her practiced discipline set the stage for female graduates of prestigious law firms two generations later being able to bring their infants to work (often in the hands of a caretaker), where they would discretely nurse them while competing with men who believed women had no place in their halls of power.

Supreme Court Justice Ginsburg (appointed by Ronald Reagan in 1969) said, "If times (the culture) were then what is now, we would have been partners in the law firm of [Justice Sandra Day] O'Connor and Ginsburg and enjoying a comfortable retirement."

Selected Ruth Bader Ginsburg quotes from those posted at mentalfloss.com by Erin McCarthy, in celebration of RBG's 84th birthday, March 2017:

> On her mother: "My mother told me two things constantly. One was to be a lady, and the other was to be independent. The study of law was unusual for women of my generation. For most girls growing up in the '40s, the most important degree was not your B.A., but your M.R.S."
> —Via ACLU

On being rejected early in her career by a firm that had already hired a woman:

> "Suppose I had gotten a job as a permanent associate. Probably I would have climbed up the ladder and today I would be a retired partner. So often in life, things that you regard as an impediment turn out to be great good fortune."
> —In conversation with Makers

> On female Supreme Court Justices: "...I'm sometimes asked when will there be enough [women on the supreme court]? And I say, 'When there are nine.' People are shocked. But there'd been nine men, and nobody's ever raised a question about that."
> —From an interview with 10th Circuit Bench & Bar Conference at the University of Colorado,

Boulder, via CBS News

On dissenting opinions: "Dissents speak to a future age. It's not simply to say, 'my colleagues are wrong, and I would do it this way,' but the greatest dissents do become court opinions."
—From an interview on *Live with Bill Maher*

On having it all: "Who—man or woman—has it all, all at once? Over my lifespan I think I have had it all. But in different periods of time things were rough. And if you have a caring life partner, you help the other person when that person needs it."
—From an interview with Katie Couric

On gender equality: "Women will have achieved true equality when men share with them the responsibility of bringing up the next generation."
—Via The Record [PDF]

On feminism: "I think the simplest explanation, and one that captures the idea, is a song that Marlo Thomas sang, 'Free to be You and Me.' Free to be, if you were a girl—doctor, lawyer, Indian chief. Anything you want to be. And if you're a boy, and you like teaching, you like nursing, you would like to have a doll, that's OK too. That notion that we should each be free to develop our own talents, whatever they may be, and not be held back by artificial barriers— manmade barriers, certainly not heaven sent."
—In conversation with Makers

On how she'd like to be remembered: "Someone who used whatever talent she had to do her work to the very best of her ability. And to help repair

14

tears in her society, to make things a little better through the use of whatever ability she has. To do something, as my colleague David Souter would say, outside myself. 'Cause I've gotten much more satisfaction for the things that I've done for which I was not paid."
—From an MSNBC interview

Christine Blasey Ford

I introduced this essay on cultural change for American women with the comment—how far we've come and how far we have to go—by looking closely at Ruth Bader Ginsburg, a girl from the not-fancy part of Brooklyn, the daughter of Russian immigrants, who in one generation evolved from a garment district bookkeeper's daughter, expected to become a high school teacher (because "how else would she earn a living?"), to a lawmaker at the pinnacle of her profession: honored and respected and affluent to boot, who got there on her own merits, as her mother encouraged her to do.

I watched Dr. Blasey Ford's testimony at the Brett Kavanaugh hearings and found it believable and moving. Her story—and her long delay in telling it—was confirmed by at least a half-dozen women who suffered assaults in childhood (by a parent or parent's friend or a brother) and in adolescence (by a neighbor) and in adulthood (by a therapist). In my practice I have treated adult women, sexually abused by therapists—fondling in one instance and intercourse in another—who blamed themselves as complicit, whose dreams and fantasies involved dangerous sexual escapades where they were the seducers of men and controlled the action, reversing helplessness into power over their aggressors. Until therapy, these women had told no one of their abuse.

All of them suffered symptoms of chronic PTSD: nightmares, disturbed ability to participate in and enjoy sex, depression and character deformation. They could function normally but in an *as-if* way. And they were vulnerable to regression triggered by life circumstances.

In short, I was not surprised at all that Dr. Ford came forward only after she saw Kavanaugh's name on a short list for a Supreme Court nomination, a position that would give him power over lives other than his own. She was 100% certain that he had assaulted her and enjoyed it, laughing at her vulnerability. (She was 15 years old at the time, and although a competitive diver, no match for a super-fit football player and basketball star.)

We know that traumatic events result in a surge of the stress hormone norepinephrine, which enhances memory. Dr. Richard A. Friedman, a psychiatrist and neuroscientist, asserts that memories formed during an assault or attack "are indelible in the way that memories of a routine day are not." He writes:

> "That's why it's credible that Christine Blasey Ford, who has accused Judge Brett Kavanaugh, President Trump's Supreme Court nominee, of sexually assaulting her when they were both teenagers, has a vivid recollection of the alleged long-ago event.
>
> "'I thought he might inadvertently kill me,' she told *The Washington Post* in a recent interview. 'He was trying to attack me and remove my clothing.'
>
> "Judge Kavanaugh has vigorously denied the charges, leading to a public debate about whether Dr. Blasey Ford's story is true. Her lawyers say she wants the F.B.I. to investigate

before she agrees to testify before the Senate. If and when she does testify, you can bet that Republican senators will try to undermine her explosive claim on the basis that the memory of an event that occurred 36 years ago must be unreliable because it happened in the distant past. If she does not testify, some of her critics will undoubtedly argue that the time that's passed is reason to doubt her recollection. Nothing could be further from the truth.

"The reason has to do with the way memories are encoded when a person is experiencing intense emotions.... That is why you can easily forget where you put your smartphone or what you had for dinner last night or last year. But you will almost never forget who raped you, whether it happened yesterday or 36 years ago. There's very little chance that you are, as some senators suggest Dr. Blasey is, 'mixed up' or 'confused.'

"It is also important to note that what Dr. Blasey is describing in her report of sexual assault by Judge Kavanaugh is not a so-called recovered memory—one that a person believes he has recalled after having suppressed it for many years. Quite the opposite: It is a traumatic memory that she's been unable to forget...."[2]

Dr. Friedman's prediction was 100% accurate. In the end, Dr. Blasey Ford was treated basely by an old boy's club (the Senate, including Susan Collins) and a President, himself accused of sexual assault by many women (which he. too denies), who had the power to instruct the FBI to pursue a limited investigation for

---

[2] Richard A. Friedman, "Opinion: Why Assault Memories Stick." The New York Times, September 19, 2018.

a political purpose: to place a Federalist-approved conservative judge on the Supreme Court for a lifetime.

I, too, was in a fraternity in college and attended keg parties, even occasionally drank too much, puked and didn't remember a lot the next morning. But I (and no one I knew) never assaulted and threatened to rape underage girls. Perhaps I traveled with adolescents and young college students who were like me and wore blinders to not see those who did? After Dr. Blasey Ford's account of being assaulted by Brett Kavanaugh, the New York Times sought stories from men who, as boys, were willing to speak about events they regretted. Several examples:

> "I have never forgotten the look on her face: she seemed at once hurt, disappointed, indignant, and bewildered." —Gene Biringer

> "I urged her to do something she rejected, and I played on our emotional entanglement until she did." —Arthur J. Slavin

> "I think 'conquering' her sexually was something I expected I needed to do." —Tom Lynch

> "I tried again and again. She didn't say no or stop. She just sat there." —Terry Wheaton[3]

Okay, point made: Brett Kavanaugh was not like me as an adolescent or student at Columbia, but he swore 100% he never assaulted 15-year-old Christine Blasey. So, he has nothing to regret except perhaps for damage to his reputation, his life being destroyed—"Yes, she was assaulted, terrible, but it wasn't me."

---

[3] "Opinion: Eight Stories of Men's Regret." The New York Times, October 19, 2018.

Dr. Blasey Ford's Story

Although both women married solid, high-achieving men who have supported them in their lives and aspirations, Christine Blasey Ford's early life could not have been more different than Ruth Bader Ginsburg's. After much on-line research, the most comprehensive description I've found—and the one that makes most clear both the differences in their upbringing and the similarities between their high achieving lives—is excerpted below, from The Washington Post (Sept 27, 2018):

> "When Donald Trump won his upset presidential victory in 2016, Christine Blasey Ford's thoughts quickly turned to a name most Americans had never heard of but one that had unsettled her for years: Brett M. Kavanaugh.

> "Kavanaugh—a judge on the prestigious U.S. Court of Appeals for the District of Columbia Circuit—was among those mentioned as a possible replacement for Supreme Court Justice Antonin Scalia, who died in 2016. When Trump nominated Neil M. Gorsuch, Ford was relieved but still uneasy.

> "Then, Justice Anthony M. Kennedy announced his retirement, and Ford, 51, began fretting again.

> "Her mind-set was, 'I've got this terrible secret.... What am I going to do with this secret?'" her husband, Russell Ford, 56, recalled.

> "To many, Kavanaugh was a respected jurist. To her, he was the teenager who had attacked her when they were in high school. Ford had already moved 3,000 miles away from the affluent Maryland suburbs where she says Kavanaugh

sexually assaulted her at a house party—a charge he would emphatically deny. Suddenly, living in California didn't seem far enough. Maybe another hemisphere would be. She went online to research other democracies where her family might settle, including New Zealand.... These were the lengths that Ford, a professor and mother of two, once considered to avoid revisiting one of her most troubling memories— one she'd discussed only in therapy and with her husband. Instead, her deeply held secret would come to dominate the headlines, putting her and her family at the center of an explosive debate about the future of the Supreme Court....

"Growing up, she was just 'Chrissy,' and in the way of younger siblings, was often described by her relationship to someone else: sister of Tom and Ralph, daughter of the older Ralph, a golf course regular who would go on to become the president of the exclusive, all-male Burning Tree Club.... Like many affluent families in the area, the Blaseys sent their children to single-gender private schools. For Ford, that meant six years at Holton-Arms, where students wore blue plaid skirts they would try to persuade their mothers to hem shorter. Her classmates included the daughters of the king of Jordan and members of the J.W. Marriott clan....

"Weekends were spent shopping at the White Flint mall, flashing fake IDs at Georgetown's Third Edition club—the drinking age was 18 then—or flocking to the house of whoever's parents were out of town to drink six-packs of Hamm's or Schaefer.

"Every summer, the 'Holton girls' would pack

into a rented house for Beach Week, an annual bacchanal of high-schoolers from around the region. The prep schools that formed Ford's overlapping social circles usually gathered at a Delaware beach town each year. Kavanaugh, in his senior-year yearbook, cited his own membership in the 'Beach Week Ralph Club.'

"Like Kavanaugh, Ford was part of that alcohol-fueled culture. But those unchaperoned parties, at beach rentals and Bethesda basements alike, frequently left the girls feeling embattled.... In her Post interview, Ford said a group of boys from Georgetown Prep was at one of the beer-drinking sessions in an unsupervised house near Columbia Country Club, possibly in the summer of 1982. One of them was Kavanaugh, whom she described as an acquaintance. At the time, she was 15, and he was 17.

Kavanaugh and his classmate Mark Judge had started drinking earlier than others, she said, and the two were 'stumbling drunk' when they pushed her into a bedroom. She alleges that Kavanaugh lay on top of her, fumbling with her clothes and pressing his hand over her mouth to keep her from screaming. Only when Judge jumped on top of them was she able to run from the room and hide until she could flee the house, she said. Her biggest fear afterward, she recalled more than 35 years later, was looking as if she had just been attacked. So, she carried herself as if she wasn't. Down the stairs. Out the door. Onto the rest of her high school years, she said. On graduation day, she wore the required white dress and carried red roses. She told no one. [Coincidentally I have chosen the cover for this book titled "Woman with Roses."—H.S.]

"It was during Ford's junior year [at UCNC Chapel Hill] when [her friend] Goldstein, who now works as an English teacher in Japan, gave her the advice that would change the course of her life. 'He said, "You're really smart, and you're just like totally [messed] up,"' Ford recalled.... If she was going to graduate on time, he said, she ought to major in psychology. The major didn't require students to take classes in a specific order, so Ford could take them all at once.

"That was how Christine Blasey Ford came to spend her life researching trauma and if it is possible to get past it."[4]

Blasey did turn her life around in California. She became a clinical psychologist, learned to surf and loved it, moved to Hawaii to complete a Ph.D., met a fellow surfer who would become her husband, switched from clinical psychology to an academic career at Stanford and—perhaps most importantly—freed herself from the country-club life and politics of her parents. She was able to tell her husband she had been physically abused. Her appreciation of the trauma she suffered—my view—led her to seek a master's degree in epidemiology at Stanford where her thesis "explored the relationship between trauma and depression," another highly adaptive way to turn passive into active mastery. She taught graduate students at Stanford and at Palo Alto University that you could recover from trauma and be stronger than you were before. Despite misgivings, she stood tall and agreed to testify face-to-face with the man she felt could have killed her; enduring the hostile interrogation of

---

[4] "Kavanaugh accuser Christine Blasey Ford moved 3,000 miles to reinvent her life. It wasn't far enough." Contrera, Shapira et al; washingtonpost.com, September 27, 2018.

senators and a hired-gun interrogator; showing herself, her husband and the students she had taught how to be strong; facing a hostile President—himself an admitted and unrepentant abuser of women—and a worldwide audience of millions, including this author—what a Hero looks and sounds like.

WOMEN IN LITERATURE: PART 2

My approach to writing, once I have an idea, is to let it germinate, or as Paul Auster (a favorite author of mine) writes, "Stories surge up out of nowhere, and if they feel compelling, you follow them. You let them unfold inside you and see where they are going to lead." At Columbia, C'59, I often studied in Butler Library with access to its millions of books. Now researching and writing "Women in Literature," I have books all over my house: in the office where I am writing on my desktop computer, in a wood-paneled den/TV room downstairs, in my psychoanalytic office downstairs, and by my bedside upstairs. Sometimes I buy a book for my library and the same book for my Kindle, so I can read it while waiting anywhere. Often, I can't find exactly the book I am looking for. But with all of my books, and the peace and quiet I didn't have at Columbia, it took me awhile to let a rather obvious idea germinate: who were my personal women heroes, past and present?

As a boy and adolescent, I had none, unless you count *Wonder Woman*, who could ward off bullets with steel wristlets and lead her band of Amazons, all in sexy bodices. My preferences were war and historical novels, biographies of male sports heroes, popular introductions to sex like *Marjorie Morningstar* and *A Stone for Danny Fisher*—hardly literary fiction with heroines like those in Jane Austen's *Pride and Prejudice*, Charlotte Bronte's *Jane Eyre*, or George Eliot's *Middlemarch*—none of them. It was not until recently as a semi-retired psychoanalyst and author that I have had the time and inclination to up my game and try *Pride and Prejudice* and *Middlemarch*. Alas, I put both of them down, only partially read.

So far, as following my proposed story-essay to explore women heroes in literature suggests, I was not actually interested in woman heroes. But maybe, I was looking in the wrong places? As the story unfolded, I thought of the Bible's Queen Esther who saved an entire population of Jews in Persia; I had played the villain Haman, the *Purimspiel* when I was a boy of about 12 years old.

Queen Esther: A Biblical Hero

The story of Esther begins with a grand banquet at the palace of King Ahasuerus, also referred to as King Xerxes (Xerxes I, who ruled Persia from 486—465 BC; in other words, about 2,500 years ago). The king, drunk on wine, commanded that his wife, Queen Vashti, come out before all the nobility and display for them her great beauty, but she refused. Ahasuerus was so angered by her disobedience that he banished her from his presence and divorced her. The king then called for a nationwide search for beautiful virgins from whom he would select his next queen.

A beautiful Jewish woman, Esther, was brought along with other young women to the citadel of Susa. When she was an orphaned child, Esther's cousin Mordecai had taken her in and raised her as his own. A man named Hegai was put in charge of preparing the women for meeting the king, a yearlong process. Esther's great beauty won her Hegai's favor and she was given special attention. She was careful, however, to not tell anyone about her nationality or family background, as her guardian Mordecai had forbidden her to do so.

When it was Esther's turn to go before King Ahasuerus, he found her the most attractive of all of the virgins and immediately placed a crown upon her head. The king held a great banquet for all of the nobles and officials to introduce her as his queen. Esther continued to hide her Jewish background, as Mordecai had warned her that it could put her life in danger.

One night, when Mordecai was sitting by the king's gate, he overheard two guards conspiring to assassinate Ahasuerus. Mordecai told Queen Esther of the plan who in turn reported it to the king, crediting Mordecai for the information. The two guards were then impaled on poles.

Soon afterwards, the king honored Haman the Agagite to an elevated position. All of the royal officials at the king's gate knelt and paid honor to Haman as the highest of all nobles, but Mordecai refused to bow down to him. When Haman found out about this, and that Mordecai was a Jew, he became enraged and wanted to kill all of the Jews of the kingdom. He convinced Ahasuerus to issue a decree to destroy all Jews, as they kept themselves separate and therefore stood in opposition to the king's rule. The king agreed, gave Haman a signet ring to keep and a promise of silver, and set a date for the Jews' annihilation.

Upon hearing of the king's plan, Mordecai took to the streets in torn garments, wailing loudly, but could only go as far as the palace gate. Esther's eunuchs and attendants told her about the king's edict and about Mordecai's strange behavior. She feared for her life and tried to avoid Mordecai's plea to approach the king to try to save the Jewish people. But Mordecai told her, "Do not think that because you are in the king's house, you alone of all the Jews will escape.... For if you remain silent, relief and deliverance for the Jews will arise from another place, but you and your father's family will perish. And who knows but that you have come to your royal position for such a time as this?"[5]

---

[5] *Esther* 4:13-4:14.

Esther responded by telling Mordecai to instruct all the Jews of Susa to join her in fasting for three days and three nights; she would then approach Ahasuerus with her request. After the three days, Esther asked that the king and Haman join her at a banquet the following day, where she would let her petition be known. The king agreed and summoned Haman, who, upon seeing Mordecai at the gate, was still so furious that his wife suggested he arrange for a pole to be set up on which to impale Mordecai the morning before the banquet.

Ahasuerus could not sleep that night and began to read the book chronicling all that had happened during his reign. While he read, the king was reminded of how Mordecai had exposed the plot to assassinate him. Wanting to reward Mordecai for his good deed, he called in Haman to ask what should be done for a man in whom the king delights. Haman thought the king was talking about himself and suggested bestowing him with extravagant gifts and honors. Haman became enraged when the king told him the man was Mordecai!

The next day at the banquet, King Ahasuerus again asked Esther to voice her request. Esther boldly asked that she and her people be spared, revealing that Haman had plotted to kill all the Jews for money. The king was furious and had Haman impaled on the very pole set up for Mordecai's death.

The king then gave Haman's estate to Queen Esther and Mordecai. They were honored with royal garments and gifts, including the signet ring the king retrieved from Haman. A decree was written and sealed to protect all Jews, giving them the right to fight to protect themselves from all enemies.

Imagine how Haman, the evil enemy of the Jews played by 12-year-old me, felt when he was booed every time his name was mentioned, and drowned out with a traditional noisemaker called a grogger!

Queen Esther, who risked her life to confront a Persian king, was a true hero. (A knowledgeable patient of mine who has often visited present-day Iran tells me that Esther's burial site is well known and can be visited to this day.)

Lady Murasaki: The Tale of Genji

The Tale of Genji is a classic work of Japanese literature, written by the noblewoman and lady-in-waiting Murasaki Shikibu (a pseudonym) in the early years of the 11th century (the original manuscript no longer exists). It is a unique depiction of the lifestyles of courtiers during the Heian period, written in archaic language and a poetics, a confusing style that makes it unreadable to the average Japanese without dedicated study.[6] It was not until the early 20th century that Genji was translated into modern Japanese; the first English translation was attempted in 1882. (I no longer have the translation I read in "Oriental Humanities"— now "Asian Studies"—during the two-semester elective I took as a senior at Columbia. The text I am re-reading is the Dover Thrift Edition, translation by Artur Waley, first published 2000 and originally published 1929, by Houghton Mifflin Co. Boston).[7]

The work recounts the life of Hikaru Genji,

---

[6] *Names, Naming, and Nature in the Tale of Genji.* Elissa Kido, Article 4, http://digitalcommons.brockport.edu. Part of the Japanese Studies Commons.

[7] See also *The Bridge of Dreams: A Poetics of the Tale of Genji.* http//www.taleofgenji.org

or "Shining Genji," the son of an ancient Japanese emperor known to readers as Emperor Kiritsubo, and a low-ranking concubine called Kiritsubo Consort. For political reasons, the emperor removes Genji from the line of succession, demoting him to a commoner by giving him the surname Minamoto, and he pursues a career as an imperial officer. The tale concentrates on Genji's romantic life and describes the customs of the aristocratic society of the time. The work is sometimes called the world's first novel, the first modern novel, the first psychological novel and the first novel still to be considered a classic. While regarded as a masterpiece, its precise classification and influence in both the Western and Eastern canons has been a matter of debate.

Following my story/essay as to where the story unfolds led me to this remarkable novel, as modern today as it was unique then. I don't recall if Professor William Theodore de Bary made the point that it was the "first psychological novel," but perhaps this essay reflects my recognition that Lady Murasaki was a hero who challenged the primacy of male writers from the Bible through antiquity. I consider her a forerunner of Virginia Woolf (*To the Lighthouse*, to be discussed later), whose poetic, free-associative, non-linear style was considered innovative and hard to understand, just as was Murasaki's 1000 years ago.

From the introduction (Dover Edition):

> Of her childhood Murasaki tells us the following anecdote: "When my brother Nobunori (the one who is now on the Board of Rites) my father was very anxious to make a good Chinese scholar of him, and often came himself to hear Nobunori read his lessons. On these occasions I was always present, and so quick was I at picking up the language that I was soon able to prompt

my brother whenever he got stuck. At this my father would sigh and say to me: If only you were a boy how happy and proud, I should be...I was careful to conceal that I (read books)...or even that I could write a single Chinese character."

Why conceal it? Chapter 2: The Broom Tree—"The Appraisal of Women on a Rainy Night"—in the Dover Edition, pages 16–43—is too long for this essay, so I will quote from the Summary, which is interesting in two regards.

1. "Genji and his brother-law...meet at Genji's palace and compare notes about women. They are joined by a guard's companions and discuss several types of women.... After Genji wakes, C. tells the story of a lover who bore his daughter but was discarded because of her meek and forgiving nature. S., a young man from the Ministry of Rites, tells the gathering of a lady who was too scholarly, preferring the rather masculine Chinese language to Japanese and *whose breath on occasion smelled of garlic* [italics mine]. The friends decide that the perfect woman should be loyal and cultured, but passive and willing to feign ignorance when the situation requires."

2. ".... The scene shifts...to where Genji is visiting his wife but finds her distant and cold...and he overhears a young lady discussing himself. He [also] meets an attractive young boy, her brother.... When everyone is asleep, Genji breaks into the lady's apartment and carries her off to his room. Leaving the next day, Genji employs the boy as a page to deliver a message to his sister, but she discourages any further relationship. He manages to see her once again but is rebuffed, leaving him to write a poem about

the inhospitable broom tree (an actual common tree in the environs that from a distance looks elegant but the closer you get the more it looks like, well, a broom). And Genji (the opportunist) sleeps with her young brother instead.

Murasaki tells her readers that a Korean sage predicts a "brilliant future for Genji and he does indeed become an uncommonly gifted young man, admired for amorous exploits with a variety of ladies…until his amorous intrigues cause a scandal at court…. [He] is banned… only to return, marry, have a daughter and settle down. His influence at court restored he becomes preoccupied with the advancement of his children and grandchildren at court, marries again—for the third time—and fathers another son." This memorable saga of Genji's great success, dishonor, redemption, serious illness and recovery leads to his adoption of the child Murasaki and as her guardian, he undertakes her education. (I am not clear if Murasaki is also Lady Murasaki, the author of this Tale. If so, this is a thoroughly modern plot device: the author becoming a character in her own novel. No wonder her court readers were confused, while enjoying every twist and turn of gossip, sex in all its variety, and a happy ending as the heroes end their lives in a Buddhist nunnery or monastery—exhausted by lives fully lived.)

There is a seamless interchange between Korean, Chinese and Japanese cultures—sages, scholars and poets—therefore this literary masterpiece cannot be understood apart from the culture at the time it was written. Nor can my essay on Women be meaningfully categorized as biological, cultural and literary. They are all are of a piece—"Utterly intertwined."[8]

A dictionary definition of heroism is taking a risk

---

[8] Sapolsky, Robert M. *Behave*. 2017, Penguin Press. Introduction, p. 7.

(of reputation or life) for a meaningful endeavor. For a woman to write a 1,000-page psychological novel, in the voice of a man with a ribald libido, when the ideal of men is that women should be "passive, loyal, cultured and willing to feign ignorance" was to risk reputation and expulsion. (See previous page, and in particular page 33 of the Dover Edition: "Sometimes indeed a woman should pretend to know less than she knows or say only a part of what she would like to say....")

This part of the story is nearly impossible to follow due to the palace intrigues, multiple characters vying for power, multiple wives and consorts; including Genji's satisfying himself with a boy—the handsome young brother of his latest infatuation, a married woman with whom he sleeps once but who then rejects him.

"Genji lay wondering what blandishments the boy might be using. He was not sanguine, for the boy was very young. Presently he came back to report his mission a failure. What an uncommonly strong woman! Genji feared he must seem a bit feckless beside her. He heaved a deep sigh. This evidence of despondency had the boy on the point of tears.

Genji sent the lady a poem:
"I wander lost in the Sonohara moorlands,
For I did not know the deceiving ways of the broom tree.
How am I to describe my sorrow?
She too lay sleepless. This was her answer:
"Here and not here, I lie in my shabby hut.
Would that I might like the broom tree vanish away."[9]

---

[9] Chapter 2, *Tale of Genji*—Exchange of Poems: Genji feels deceived by her refusal to sleep with him again—like the prickly broom tree seen from afar is attractive, but up-close is prickly, like the woman who refuses his love, which is no more than a role in the hay to him. She feels lonely and ashamed. She accepts the role of victim and

What, you may wonder, does this have to do with my thesis of the author Lady Murasaki as a hero? Well, before there was D.H. Lawrence's *Lady Chatterley's Lover*, Anais Nin's journals and *Delta of Venus,* a book of 15 short stories published posthumously in 1977 (though largely written in the 1940s as erotica for a private collector) and not to be ignored, her lover Henry Miller's *Tropic of Cancer* (1934)...there was Lady Murasaki.

The Goddess Athena

My idiosyncratic choice of women heroes led me to Athena, who in myth was a contemporary of Lady Murasaki (12th Century B.C.). This choice was more than anything else based on my wanting an opportunity to publish again a poem by Homer (see below) of Odysseus' homecoming after ten years of wandering after his victory in the Trojan War, including finally, seven years as captive to the allure and seduction of Calypso, a nymph-daughter of Zeus. Odysseus was a favorite of Athena (similar character traits, both tricksters) who intervened on his behalf with Zeus to control the fury of Poseidon, her nemesis, so that he was not drowned at sea and survived Poseidon's storms, returning safely to Ithaca and to his abandoned son Telemachus and faithful wife Penelope. (Notice as in Genji's tale that the ideal woman is loyal and defers to her husband, except that Penelope is a strong woman in her own right by resisting the entreaties of the horde of men who want to bed her while her husband is bedding Calypso. What's ancient is forever new.)

"Penelope tests Odysseus and when he passes

---

he feels victimized by her. "Oh well," he thinks, "I'll sleep with her brother."

the 'bed test'...she recognizes her wayward hero and takes him to the comfort of their bed, a bed literally rooted to the earth, a description of this 'home coming' in metaphoric but unmistakable language as an extended primal scene arranged and enjoyed by the Gods because it pleased them to honor Odysseus and his ever-loyal wife. Or perhaps just because the Gods too were part human and recognized the ecstasy of the primal urge for sexual pleasure that was at the same time inseparable from a long maternal embrace that ushers in a new day/life for us all." —David Denby, a movie critic who, while sitting in the Great Books course he took at Columbia (as did I), has become the professor, making his point by quoting this Homeric masterpiece:[10]

And as when the land appears welcome to men who are swimming, after Poseidon has smashed their strong-built ships on the open water, pounding it with the weight of wind and the heavy seas, and only a few escape the gray water landward by swimming with a thick scurf of salt coated upon them, and gladly they set foot upon the shore, escaping the evil; so welcome was her husband to her as she looked upon him, and she would not let him go from the embrace of her white arms. Now Dawn of the rosy fingers would have dawned on their weeping, had not the grey-eyed goddess Athena planned it otherwise. She held the long night back at the outward edge, she detained Dawn of the golden throne by the Ocean and would not let her harness her fast-footed horses who bring the daylight to people: Lampos and Phaeton, the

---

[10] Denby, David. *Great Books: My Adventures with Homer, Rousseau, Woolf and other Indestructible Writers of the Western World.* 1996, Simon & Schuster. Ch. 4, The Odyssey, p. 86.

Dawn's horses, who carry her.... Then resourceful Odysseus spoke to his wife, saying: 'Dear wife, we have not yet come to the limit of all our trials....

Odysseus soon slaughtered the suitors who had feasted at his expense but had never violated his wife. He slaughtered the servant girls who satisfied the men and themselves, as was acceptable behavior at the time, which Odysseus well knew. But what if his rage was fueled by the posttraumatic stress of years of killing and his secret addiction to that killing? How could he be at peace in his wife's forgiving, loving arms when he craved the excitements of war? I cannot but think that Odysseus too suffered from PTS (like Achilles), a malady that existed but had not yet been named.

A more personal reason to write of Athena was a fond recollection of a trip with my wife to Athens as part of a cruise from Istanbul to Ephesus, and then to the islands of Mykonos, Rhodes and Santorini, ending in Athens, where my wife and I spent three nights.

Lady Murasaki was an actual person as was Queen Esther, while Athena was part human and part goddess. The heroes of antiquity have survived because they serve our need for them to provide a mirror for us to see ourselves as we are and as we may wish to be.

It's time to leap forward to Tolstoy's *Anna Karenina* and then into the 20th century to Virginia Woolf's Mrs. Ramsey, and finally to land in our 21st century with Laureen Graff's most recent book of short stories, *Florida.*

Anna Karenina: **Leo Tolstoy (1873–77)**

Happy families are all alike; every unhappy family is unhappy in its own way.
—Tolstoy

Several years ago, I determined to read classic novels I had never read in college or during my post-college years. I put them on a bucket list along with my usual overcrowded reading schedule. The first was *Moby-Dick* and the second was *Anna Karenina*. Both have classic first sentences: "Call me Ishmael" and "Happy families..." that draw you into the story. (Ishmael is the narrator and not a character; see Wikipedia.)[11]

Joshua Rothman, after seeing the premier of the latest film version of *Anna Karenina*, wrote in *The New Yorker* (Nov 12, 2012),

> "...if you know and love the novel, something about the movie just doesn't feel right. The problem, I think, is that it's too romantic. The film, as Wright, the Director, promised, is all about love, but Tolstoy's 'Anna Karenina' isn't a love story. If anything, 'Anna Karenina' is a warning against the myth and cult of love.

---

[11] From Wikipedia: "Ishmael, the only surviving crewmember of the Pequod, is the narrator of the book. His importance relies on his role as narrator; as a character, he is only a minor participant in the action and the main protagonist is Captain Ahab. The Biblical name has come to symbolize orphans, exiles, and social outcasts.

"Because he was the first person narrator, most of the criticism of Moby-Dick either confused Ishmael with the author himself or overlooked him. From the mid-twentieth century onward, critics distinguished Ishmael from Melville, establishing the character's mystic and speculative consciousness as a central force in contrast to Ahab's monomaniacal force of will."

"When I first started reading Anna Karenina,'
ten years ago...I, too, thought of it as a love
story. I was twenty-three, and thinking of
getting married; to me, it was obvious that the
novel was about love, good and bad, wise and
unwise. I read the novel as you might read any
novel about marriage and adultery. You think
about the protagonists and their choices; you
root for happy endings.... But this love-story
idea of love isn't really native to 'Anna Karenina.'
Tolstoy, when he wrote the novel, was thinking
about love in a different way, as a kind of fate, or
curse, or judgment, and as a vector by which the
universe distributes happiness and unhappiness,
unfairly and apparently at random.

"Those thoughts aren't very romantic, but
they are Tolstoyan. When he turned to 'Anna
Karenina,' Tolstoy didn't simply leave behind
the themes of 'War and Peace.' Instead, he found
a way of thinking about many of same issues that
had always interested him—fate, chance, our
powerlessness against circumstances and our
determination to change them—in a different
context. In 1873, when Tolstoy began writing
'Anna Karenina,' he was in the midst of planning
a historical novel about Peter the Great."

Hawthorne wrote *The Scarlet Letter* in 1860. Might
Tolstoy have come upon a French translation, or is it
coincidence that Anna fits the Scarlet profile?

Rothman continues:

"Starting in 1870, [Tolstoy] had shut himself up
in his study, reading and making notes.... Peter
the Great turned out to be too epic a subject
even for Tolstoy. ('I am in a very bad mood,'

37

he wrote to a friend. 'Making no headway. The project I have chosen is incredibly difficult. There is no end to the preliminary research, the outline is swelling out of all proportion and I feel my strength ebbing away.')"

I've had that thought about this book as well.

"Tolstoy needed a more manageable subject. Then he discovered something: another way into his concerns that wasn't overblown and historical, but personal, intimate, and sad. In his biography of Tolstoy, Henri Troyat explains the novel's origins this way:[12]

"'Suddenly he had an illumination.... A neighbor and friend of his, Bibikov, the snipe hunter, lived with a woman named Anna Stepanovna Pirogova.... But he had been neglecting her of late for his children's German governess.... Learning of his treachery, Anna Stepanovna's jealousy burst all bounds; she ran away, carrying a bundle of clothes, and wandered about the countryside for three days, crazed with grief. Then she threw herself under a freight train at the Yasenki station. Before she died, she sent a note to Bibikov: 'You are my murderer. Be happy, if an assassin can be happy. If you like you can see my corpse on the rails at Yasenki.' .... The following day Tolstoy had gone to the station as a spectator, while the autopsy was being performed in the presence of a police inspector. Standing in a corner of the shed,

---

[12] Review of Troyat's book on Amazon: "Leo Tolstoy embodies the most extraordinary contradictions. He was a wealthy aristocrat who preached the virtues of poverty and the peasant life, a misogynist who wrote *Anna Karenina*, and a supreme writer who declared, 'Literature is rubbish.' From Tolstoy's famously bad marriage to his enormously successful career, Troyat presents a brilliant portrait that reads like an epic novel written by Tolstoy himself."

he had observed every detail of the woman's body lying on the table, bloody and mutilated, with its skull crushed. How shameless, he thought, and yet how chaste. A dreadful lesson was brought home to him by that white, naked flesh, those dead breasts, those inert thighs that had felt and given pleasure. He tried to imagine the existence of this poor woman who had given all for love, only to meet with such a trite, ugly death."

Rothman's long discussion addresses and debunks my point of view as irrelevant, more the point of view of students he has taught, relativistic and not Tolstoy's point of view (that love is a kind of fate, or curse, or judgment, and a vector by which the universe distributes happiness and unhappiness, unfairly and apparently at random). But I disagree. Anna knew that if she chose to have an affair with Vronsky, she might lose everything—even her children—because she was not merely in love, but *passionately* in love and willing to risk all to be with him. But Vronsky betrayed her love and had an affair that led to despair: "I'd be better off dead" (than to live this way).

Does fate or God play a hand in all this? Well, no. Anna announced her infatuation. She was aroused by Vronsky's magnificent horsemanship. (Her kind of man—not the intellectual, safe civil servant Karenin whom she tried to love but couldn't.) Does Tolstoy think chance and coincidence play a role in life? Sure, who doesn't?

Anna meets Vronsky on a train and moves in on him when Vronsky does not respond to Kitty's overtures. What is the symbolism of trains, which is not spelled out by Tolstoy? Stephen Grosz in *The Examined Life* (W.B. Norton and Co, UK, 2013) wrote a clinical vignette titled, "You can't get somewhere unless you leave somewhere"—especially in Russia, I would add, a vast country where trains were part of life—and for Anna, a train was also an over-determined symbol of her wish to escape from the pain she suffered, risking all. Tolstoy, in the omniscient voice, recognizes Anna's (unladylike) rage at Vronsky and her own guilt, only to be satisfied in Biblical fashion by train; and revenge against the lover who betrayed her. As she utters or thinks: "Vengeance is mine; I will repay."

Coda:

The laudanum given to Anna by Vronsky, who wanted to relieve her suffering chemically rather than by his love, may have had the side effect of visual hallucinations. Her throwing herself on the tracks may have been a toxic paranoid psychosis. The reader is left to decide. So much of life is a mystery for Tolstoy and us.

Is Anna a hero? On balance, I believe she was. She made a choice and suffered the consequences socially and morally. In another time—like now—with the support of other women and less harsh divorce laws, mediated custody disputes, alimony, more jobs for single women and more opportunities to remarry, as well as medication and psychotherapy for depression, Tolstoy might not have written this magnificent, complex tragedy.

After Stephen Grosz: privacy concerns preclude me from providing clinical data about successful suicides: lying in front of trains, taking poison, hanging, overdosing on insulin and perhaps the cruelest of all, suicide on the anniversary/birthday of a widowed spouse. "Vengeance is mine. I will repay."

To the Lighthouse: Virginia Woolf (1927)

If there remains any question about Anna Karenina being a hero or a victim of fate (or of her culture) for making what turned out to be a wrong decision, this essay on Virginia Woolf's novel *To the Lighthouse* will raise similar questions.

I am reminded of a scene in Stephen Sondheim's musical, *Into the Woods*. (A bit long, but a moral tale you can read about in the footnote.[13]) When Rapunzel of the long golden hair chooses to marry the Prince, who in return will rescue her from the tower where she has been imprisoned for stealing the sorceress's Rapunzel or "bell flower," the audience recognizes the foppish prince as a bad choice and screams, "No, no," but she does marry him.

The sorceress, played in scary witch's makeup by Bernadette Peters à la Ethel Merman in the original 1987 Broadway production, reminds Rapunzel why she is in the tower hidden away: to devote all her time spinning straw into gold and not wasting her time on men. Rapunzel replies as the foppish prince approaches, "How would I know a good man from a bad man?" He climbs up her hair, and down with her. But there is no happy ending in this fairy tale marriage.

Anna Karenina chose knowingly but denied Vronsky's true character because of passion. Virginia Woolf's Mrs. Ramsay married a man much like the author's father. (Woolf acknowledged that she based Mr. and Mrs. Ramsay on her parents. Her husband, Leonard Woolf, was an "ex-colonial administrator, writer and political thinker." He was knighted in 1902 as an eminent man of letters. Her mother epitomized the Victorian

---

[13] https://germanstories.vcu.edu/grimm/rapunzel_e.html

ideal of femininity.) But both Anna and Mrs. Ramsay were constrained by their cultures. Mrs. Ramsay married a man not unlike Anna's first husband, Count Alexei Alexandrovich Karenin, a senior government official.

Anna Dang's essay, "Farewell, Mrs. Ramsay: a closer look at the gender dynamics in *To the Light House* (1917)"[14] is well worth reading but does not to do justice to this masterpiece of modernity.

Excerpts from "Farewell, Mrs. Ramsay:"

Men come from Mars

The characters...thus adhere to an age-old distinction between the sexes: while Ulysses goes off on wild adventures, Penelope spends her days quietly weaving (here, the intricate tapestry has been replaced by the stocking that Mrs. Ramsay weaves for the lighthouse keeper's son). At first glance, the men of the novel seem nothing like the armor-clad heroes of ancient Greek epics: they appear to be stuffy, socially awkward characters, absorbed in their dissertations. But for Mr. Ramsay, this discrepancy is irrelevant; he sees his philosophy books as part of the search of the human mind for truth, and himself as a metaphorical "leader of a doomed expedition" encroaching upon the coast of unknown lands (p. 46). In contrast, the restfulness of domestic life is somewhat of a novelty for him—certainly simpler, more trivial than his bold endeavors into the depths of human knowledge, but undeniably seductive. Mr. Ramsay's attraction to domestic bliss is reflected in his comical fascination for a "pretty" hen and its chicklets crossing the

---

[14] https://www.linkedin.com/pulse/farewell-mrs-ramsay-closer-look-gender-dynamics-virginia-anna-dang/

road.... After a lifetime of academic exploits, the weary husband resignedly "bends his head" to the "lovely and unfamiliar" profiles of his wife and son (p. 46), like Ulysses coming back to his native Ithaca after twenty years at sea."

And women from Venus

The same things that fascinate the men seem to repel the women. At the beginning of the novel, Mrs. Ramsay expresses her concern for the men staying inside the lighthouse: she deplores their loneliness and vulnerability, trying to elicit the compassion of her daughters especially (p. 11). In the second half of the novel, we learn that her husband feels interest—and perhaps even envy—for the heroic fishermen struggling to survive at sea. Women are not "sailors and adventurers" (p. 119); if anything, they are creators. In contrast to the dryness and "fatal sterility" of Mr. Ramsay (p. 47), Mrs. Ramsay is portrayed as a symbol of life, warmth, and "delicious fecundity.... While her husband works with abstract concepts, she prefers to work with people, creating friendships and happiness. During dinner, Mrs. Ramsay becomes acutely aware of the disharmony between her guests.... Despite her own exhaustion, she engages in friendly banter to try and turn this random collection of strangers into a coherent whole. She wholeheartedly accepts that this is her responsibility as a woman and as a hostess, "for if she did not do it nobody would do it" (p. 99).... Interestingly, this kind of "female" creativity is associated with Lily Briscoe's artistic creativity: both the homemaker and the painter are able to freeze a moment in eternity.

This association draws a link between Lily's two major insecurities: she worries that she cannot be a successful painter (a concern worsened by Charles Tansley's taunt that "women can't paint, women can't write") and is frustrated by her belief that she is not a real "woman", but only a "dried-up old maid" (p. 175).

It was actually shocking to read "Farewell, Mrs. Ramsay" after having written about Queen Esther, who stood up to Ahasuerus only after fasting, praying and following the direction of Mordecai; about Lady Murasaki who was smarter than her brother, knowing her father would feel "oh, so proud if he had a son" and expressed her boldness, cleverness and assertive sexuality through the golden boy Genji, the hero of her novel; and about Athena, who lured Odysseus away from Calypso to return him to faithful Penelope (who, like Rapunzel, spends her days weaving but is attracted to a bold Prince); and about the bold Anna who risked everything and lost. I needed to set limits on my theme of "Women in Literature" by seeking to find heroism in them, like the heroism of Ruth Bader Ginsburg and Christine Blasey Ford; but my unconscious bias toward maleness has turned to disappointment in the men who, out of envy and fear of the power of women, see empathy as weakness: discount as accouterments, not necessities, the aesthetics of a delicious meal, a beautifully set table and the comfort of guests facilitated by a caring hostess, as compared to the aggressive actions of men—while Mrs. Ramsey who, in deference or exhaustion, looks down and keeps peace in her family by averting her gaze.

I am aware that I oversimplify; all men are not warriors, boors or misogynists, nor do all women live to please men and mask their intelligence so as not to threaten and lose them. It is now 2019, not 1010, or 1870,

44

or 1927. Women are and have long been world leaders (including but not limited to Indira Gandhi, Benazir Bhutto, Sahle-Work Zewde of Ethiopia, Margaret Thatcher, Corazon Aquino, Theresa May, Golda Meir, Angela Merkel, Hillary Clinton who ran for President of the United States in 2016 and those now in the running as of this writing). Half of the professional schools— law, medicine—that were 90% male not so long ago now boast enrollments that are 50% or greater female. (And women shop for wine, just like men.) Most of the world has changed, but not all of it. (I have tried to avoid politics in this essay, but all that I have written about culture or even biology is political (see Sapolsky again.) For example, when Watson and Crick stole the plans for the double helix model for DNA from the desk of a female researcher, they won fame and fortune while she, Rosalind Franklin, is but a footnote in the history of science.

But enough. I want to explore the relationship between Mr. and Mrs. Ramsay, so different from each other yet able to form a new form of intimacy: the mystery of the thing they share, the space they respect and allow each other, which must give way to new forms of engagement that shun sentimentality and celebrate spontaneity of expression...new complex symbols (like the Lighthouse that both hypnotizes and can be counted on—the beat of the third sweep—to sweep Mrs. Ramsay's unconscious, to challenge those of adventurous spirit (willing to risk drowning or disappointment)...that it is, after all, only a stark, cold, lonely place, and the father and son who live there are dependent on visitors for tobacco, warm socks and uneaten sandwiches, until they can bear it no longer and must leave —as we must all give up what we can no longer bear and join those shipwrecked sailors who have drowned in the sea. (More Mrs. Ramsay's view than her husband's, who celebrates the heroism of those who risk death and deprivation and insists, tyrannically, that at least two of his children, Cam and James—sister and brother—, accompany him on a difficult sail, with James at the helm while Mr. Ramsay eats a sandwich and reads, James craving recognition and intimacy. The siblings make a pact to resist the tyrant they have learned to hate.)[15]

The Introduction

I am partial to reading the introduction to special museum exhibits designed to provide the interested audience with a brief orientation (historical and particular) to what they are about to see; and to renting audio guides to enrich my viewing experience. At a 2016 Jackson Pollack exhibit at the Museum of Modern Art, New York, the first work, displayed on a small wall before the more familiar outsized drip paintings awaiting beyond, was a small, drab, unremarkable student painting (Art Students League, 1930) that spoke to me without words: *What lies ahead is a leap into modernism,* although at that moment I would not have thought of it that way.

From the Pollock MoMA introduction:

"In 1947 Jackson Pollock arrived at a new mode of working that brought him international fame. His method consisted of flinging and dripping thinned enamel paint onto an unstretched canvas laid on the floor of his studio. This direct, physical engagement with his materials welcomed gravity, velocity, and improvisation

---

[15] I have, for the sake of the flow of this complicated-non-linear novel, and in the spirit of its author, avoided page references and conflated scenes from different sections of the book. It follows my own stream of consciousness—free associations—which is how I both write and practice psychoanalysis.

46

into the artistic process, and allowed line and color to stand alone, functioning entirely independently of form. His works, which came to be known as 'drip paintings,' present less a picture than a record of the fluid properties of paint itself."

What, dear reader, you might ask, does this have to do with the introduction to *To the Lighthouse*?

Herewith, excerpts from the Wordsworth Edition by Dr. Bradbury[16] who provides the author's intent to write a modern (art) form of writing (*The Diary of Virginia Woolf*, The Hogarth Press, London):

May 15, 1925: **Woolf in her diary:** "Mother and father's character complete, childhood...all the usual things...life and death...."

Bradbury: "Two months later, she notes 'possible branches and roots which I do not perceive now...something else I'm dared to do by my friends [The Bloomsbury Group—London—of artists, poets authors and intellectuals] which has no name 'this impersonal thing' that signals the modernism of *To the Lighthouse*... the personal and autobiographical is caught up in a cultural shift from one era to another, new possibilities (especially for women) that requires new forms, rhythms and modes of expression... art as a dynamic field not static design...."

Bradbury: "What Woolf wished to get hold of was that very jar on the nerves, the thing itself before it has been made anything."

---

[16] 1994, with Introduction and Notes by Dr. Nicola Bradbury added 2002.

Jackson Pollock's paintings at first jarred my nerves because they were a new form of art painted to the varied, spontaneous rhythms of jazz; not, as some critics harped, something any child with finger paints could do as well.

Bradbury alerts us that Mrs. Ramsay (*Diary*, November 1928) "means to eliminate all waste, deadness, superfluity, to give the moment whole, whatever it includes." That was the challenge I (author) took seriously. It meant that I had to read carefully. And it reminded me of my favorite philosopher, Michel de Montaigne who in 1570 published his Essays in exactly the same way. (The very well-read Woolf and her literary friends certainly knew of Montaigne and conceivably envisioned a new, spontaneous, introspective form: the non-linear novel.) As noted by Bradbury, Woolf envisioned, on the dare of her friends, "the flight of time & the consequent break in unity in my design.... I conceive the book in three parts interests me very much."

It also interested Tolstoy, who was both a progressive rebel against the norms of his elite class and an early feminist who shunned a happy, romantic ending for bold Anna (while providing her sister Kitty with Levin, a progressive land-owning farmer), instead writing a suicide by train. Woolf's Mrs. Ramsay suicided by drowning; but both women—at least in part as reactions against the power of men they admired—loved but held themselves to be inferior to men, which of course they were not; different, yes, but not inferior It just occurred to me that Lily Briscoe, who remains an old maid and envies the fecundity of Mrs. Ramsay (whom she also loves but with whom she feels competitive for the love of Mr. Ramsay), is also an analogue for Tolstoy's Anna. (Analogue is used in literary history in two related senses: a work which resembles another in terms of one or more motifs, characters, scenes, phrases or events; or a phrase which resembles one found in another work.) Lily takes to heart an older man's view (Mr. Banks, a father figure) that woman cannot produce important art; she won't show him the painting she is working on and of course Mrs. Ramsay isn't even invited to journey to the Lighthouse but can provide food and a warm scarf for the keeper's son. (There are online blogs devoted to scholarly discussions of both these master works that are beyond me and the scope of this essay.)

The editors of the Wordsworth Edition suggest that the text be read with fresh eyes before the Introduction, which may work for some but not for me. What interested me most was the "mystery of the thing" between the Ramsays and the effect on their children "who remember everything"; the sudden death of Mrs. Ramsay in Part Two; and role of Lily Briscoe in Part Three.

Part 1

Mr. Ramsay's mantra is:

The Charge of the Light Brigade
by Alfred, Lord Tennyson

I
Half a league, half a league,
Half a league onward,
All in the Valley of Death
Rode the six hundred.
"Foreward, the Light Brigade!
Charge for the guns!" he said.
Into the Valley of Death
Rode the six hundred.

II

"Forward, the Light Brigade!"
Was there a man dismayed?
Not though the soldier knew
Someone had blundered.
Theirs not to make reply,
Theirs not to reason why,
Theirs but to do and die.
Into the valley of Death
Rode the six hundred.

III

Cannon to right of them,
Cannon to left of them,
Cannon in front of them
Volleyed and thundered;
Stormed at with shot and shell,
Boldly they rode and well,
Into the jaws of Death,
Into the mouth of hell
Rode the six hundred.

IV

Flashed all their sabres bare,
Flashed as they turned in air
Sabring the gunners there,
Charging an army, while
All the world wondered.
Plunged in the battery-smoke
Right through the line they broke;
Cossack and Russian
Reeled from the sabre stroke
Shattered and sundered.
Then they rode back, but not
Not the six hundred.

V
Cannon to right of them,
Cannon to left of them,
Cannon behind them
Volleyed and thundered;
Stormed at with shot and shell,
While horse and hero fell.
They that had fought so well
Came through the jaws of Death,
Back from the mouth of hell,
All that was left of them,
Left of six hundred.

VI
When can their glory fade?
O the wild charge they made!
All the world wondered.
Honour the charge they made!
Honour the Light Brigade,
Noble six hundred!

Mrs. Ramsay reads a story to James, whom she recognizes as a kindred spirit, a sad, ironic Grimm's fairy tale (summarized in the after Notes: "A poor fisherman catches and releases a 'Golden Flounder,' a prince in disguise. His wife nags him to ask the fish for ever greater rewards until the Golden Flounder returns them to their original poverty.") This is indeed a strange tale to read to James and cries for interpretation: children sense dysfunction in a family and James knows that his father is not the prince his mother thought she married. She can't nag him to be who he is not and she is punished for wanting more from him by remaining with him in their impoverished marriage (my interpretation).

In the text, Mrs. Ramsay is knitting, picks up a book and reads at random a poem:

"And all the lives we ever lived
And all the lives to be,
Are full of trees and changing leaves.

"...she felt she was climbing upwards, backwards, shoving her way up under petals that curved around her, so that she only knew this is white, or this is red...she read and turned the page, zigzagging this way and that...until a little sound roused her, her husband slapping his thighs.... Don't interrupt me, he seemed to be saying....

"Mrs. Ramsay raised her head and like a person in a light sleep seemed to say that if he wanted her to wake she would, she really would, but otherwise, might she go on sleeping, just a little longer, just a little longer? She was climbing up those branches, this way and that, laying hands on one flower and then another.

"Nor praise the deep vermillion in the rose"

"How satisfying! How restful!... But she was becoming conscious of her husband looking at her. He was smiling at her, quizzically, as if he were ridiculing her gently for being asleep in broad daylight, but at the same time he was thinking, Go on reading. You don't look sad now, he thought. And he wondered what she was reading, and exaggerated her ignorance, her simplicity, for he liked to think that she was not clever, not book-learned at all. He wondered if she understood what she was reading. Probably not...[but] she was astonishingly beautiful."

She takes up her knitting and talks (about Paul and Minta becoming engaged, which she had encouraged).

"He snorted. He felt about this engagement as

he always felt about any engagement; the girl is much too good for that young man. Slowly it came into her head, why is it then that one wants people to marry? What was the value, the meaning of things? (*Every word they said now would be true.*) [Emphasis mine. There it is, the truth, almost an aside.]

Do say something, she thought wishing only to hear his voice. The thing folding them in was beginning, she felt, to close round her again. Say anything, she begged, looking at him as if for help.... He was silent, swinging the compass on his watch chain to and fro, and thinking of Scott's novels and Balzac's novels... coming side by side, quite close, she could feel his mind like a raised hand....

"You won't finish that stocking tonight," he said, pointing to her stocking. That was what she wanted—the asperity in his voice reproving her. If he says it's wrong to be pessimistic probably it is wrong, she thought; the marriage will turn out all right. "No," she said, flattening the stocking out upon her knee, "I shan't finish it."

As Part One closed I felt deeply sad. Mr. Ramsay needs to lead the Charge—to Do and Die—and the victor goes the prize, everlasting fame and a beautiful woman who can't say she loves him but needs his asperity. But she needs more. She needs to be valued not only for her beauty—which at age 50 is beginning to fade—as will the perfect table flowers fade and the perfect fruit bowl rot if left uneaten (a key dinner scene I leave for you to read); and to know their children who will not be young forever: the beautiful Prue he doesn't notice or the promising mathematician, Andrew, who needs love even if he doesn't win a scholarship (not that with eight kids to educate on an academic's income some money wouldn't be helpful)...and as Mrs. Ramsay keeps reminding herself and him, the green house will cost "fifty pounds," a lot of money that they don't have to spare. And she needs poetry, dreams and appreciation for her keen intellect, bookishness and generosity. Lily Briscoe, the spinster artist who will never marry or have any children because she is not beautiful and will not allow in any men who might love her—the older botanist Mr. Bankes (who Mrs. Ramsay hopes will marry Lily), the misogynist Mr. Tansey, who disparages her talents— because her painting (herself) isn't perfect; the tree isn't in the right place. "She would move the tree rather more to the middle," away from the "degradation," as she calls it, of marriage.

All of "this mystery of the thing" exists as Woolf, the modernist, is making the case for new forms of art, poetry, novels, music, marriage, childrearing, politics— everything—while also eulogizing the dynamics and forms that live on and demand to be heard as well. The regularity of the sweep of the lighthouse beam is contrasted with the uncertainty of the weather and waves, life itself; and our unconscious minds—Freud and Horney with what Homer has to teach us about our unconscious drives—classical art and music with drip paintings and jazz; and war—always war—to be fought, not with charging horses and men with swords, but with tanks and cannons and women fighting alongside men flying helicopters. (Why not fast forward to the present.)

No, everything will not turn out all right.

Part Two: Time Passes

Woolf writes: The summer house is being closed

for the winter. The lamps are extinguished "except that Mr. Carmichael, who liked to lie awake a little reading Virgil, kept his candle burning rather longer than the rest." An empty house; darkness creeps in; the wallpaper crumbles; there are no children; the leaves are falling, and winter is upon the land and the flood of darkness creeps in; the desolate house smells of death. "Mr. Ramsay, stumbling along a passage one dark morning, stretched his arms out, but Mrs. Ramsay having died rather suddenly the night before, his arms, though stretched out, remained empty."

This passage seems out of place and awkward, but perhaps, purposely so, it's meant to shock us. No explanation; the detritus of sudden departure left behind as though no one would return next summer. The allusions to war are unmistakable. Old Mrs. McNab does her best to sweep the dust because someone must be alive as she receives monthly checks, although no one calls or visits. Then, Spring returns and "it was impossible to resist the strange intimation which every gull, flower, tree, man and woman, and the white earth itself seemed to declare (but if questioned at once to withdraw) that good triumphs, happiness prevails, order rules..." With its promise of regeneration, "the spring with her bees humming and gnats dancing threw her cloak about her, veiled her eyes, averted her head, and among passing shadows and flights of small rain seemed to have taken upon her a knowledge of the sorrows of mankind." And then we learn: Prue—the beautiful—has married—and died in childbirth. And "A shell exploded. Twenty or thirty young men were blown up in France, among them Andrew Ramsay, whose death, mercifully, was instantaneous."

Mother nature is the hero of this story and Virginia Woolf the narrator of her story. The form is modern, but the plot line is as old as our species and as reassuring as a mother—Mrs. Ramsay—who holds James to her bosom and holds out hope: maybe it—the weather—will be fine; she strokes his head and reads him the strange story of the Golden Flounder. Mrs. McNab and a friend clean the house; flowers are put in the rooms, but some of the Brigade have died and cannot return. Mrs. Ramsay rejects her husband's pessimism, but is worn down by him, and as we are not told but are certain nonetheless, drowns herself in the sea—the water from which we all emerge.

Part Three: The Lighthouse

Ten years have passed, and Lily Briscoe is invited to a reunion. She wonders, what does it mean then, what can it all mean? "For really, what did she feel, come back after all these years and Mrs. Ramsay dead? Nothing, nothing—nothing that she could express at all."

But then she does express, if not all meaning, because people and nature are mysteries that change when viewed from different perspectives. Much that can remain constant: her love for Mrs. Ramsay, her muse and foil (Mrs. Ramsay writes hundreds of letters and cares for her family and guests, brings food and companionship to people in town, while she—Lily—has not finished the painting she started ten years ago); and her love for Mr. Ramsay (safer for her to admit now that Mrs. Ramsay is dead).

We learn what Lily learns about the nature of character that is consistent over time, for example that some people are better off not marrying; about the creative process itself (art and writing); about the process of mourning, aging and dying; and coming to terms with childhood injuries that with the perspective of time yield to the recognition of residual love for what was once hated (most importantly the tyranny of Mr. Ramsay toward his children—Cam and James standing for all their siblings, including Prue and Andrew—mourned but not forgotten).

Lily becomes more empathic toward Mrs. Ramsay as she senses her own conflicting feelings for Mr. Ramsay: the power of his physical attraction and the pain she feels when he does not pay attention to her, his demand for sympathy by acting the victim of his wife's death ("the missing something" between them that was established when she said she would marry him but did not say till Love do us part). He is still deeply insecure but imperious, even as an old but still handsome man standing in the bow of the sailboat in which he has insisted that James, his youngest son, and Cam, his lively, adventurous daughter who longs for his attention, to join him to (finally) visit the Lighthouse (although they have vowed to resist the tyrant, who true to form reads a book and pays them no attention on the somewhat perilous sail across the open sea to the rocky island on which many shops have foundered and sailors drowned.)

On page 150 of the Wordsworth edition, James saw his bareheaded father, "exposed to everything. He looked very old...like some old stone lying on the sand, he looked as if he had become physically what was always at the back of both of their minds—that loneliness which was for both of them the truth about things." And on the last two pages, 153–154, as their father is looking back toward their summer home—the children's childhood, their past—"With his long-sighted eyes perhaps he could see the dwindled leaf-like shape standing on end on a plate of gold quite clearly. What could he see? Cam wondered." (She who could not remain the tyrant in arms with her brother because she had loved her father as a child for the same qualities her mother had loved in him-—his do and die strength, intellectual brilliance, his asperity, and his neediness.) And James, sensing what Cam thought, *his father's fragility as he sat*:

> "bareheaded with his parcel on his knee staring and staring at the frail blue shape which seemed like the vapour of something that had burnt itself away. What do you want? they both wanted to ask. They both wanted to say, Ask us anything and we will give it you. But he did not ask them anything. He sat and looked at the island and he might be thinking, *We perished, each alone, or he might be thinking, I have reached it. I have found it; but he said nothing.*

> Then he put on his hat.

"'Bring those parcels,' he said, nodding his head at the things Nancy had done up for them to take to the Lighthouse. 'The parcels for the Lighthouse men,' he said. *He rose and stood in the bow of the boat, very straight and tall, for all the world*, James thought, as if he were saying, 'There is no God,' and Cam thought, as if he were leaping into space, and they both rose to follow him as he sprung lightly like a young man, holding his parcel, on to the rock."

> "'He must have reached it,' said Lily Briscoe, aloud, feeling suddenly completely tired out. For the Lighthouse had become almost invisible, had melted away into a blue haze... Whatever she had wanted to give him, when he left her that morning, she had given him at last."

Lily recalled realizing how much Mrs. Ramsay had loved her husband; she couldn't give him words, but she could give him her green shawl because she knew he needed something...and it wearied her (Mrs. Ramsay)... he would say her name and once again, but still she held back and then she would go to him, with such dignity as there had been in their relationship. Lily must hold the scene so, in a vice, and let nothing spoil it: to be on a level with ordinary experience, to feel simply that's a chair, that's a table, and yet at the same time it's a miracle, it's an ecstasy. Lily wanted Mrs. Ramsay, whom she loved and...she holding her brush went to the edge of the lawn. Where was that boat now? Mr. Ramsay? She wanted him (she had given him her love at last). She returned to her canvas.

> "There it was—her picture. Yes, with all its greens and blues, its lines running up and across, its attempt at something. It would be hung in the attics, she thought; it would be destroyed. But what did that matter? she asked herself, taking up her brush again. She looked at the steps; they were empty; she looked at her canvas; it was blurred. With a sudden intensity, as if she saw it clear for a second, she drew a line there, in the centre. It was done; it was finished. Yes, she thought, laying down her brush in extreme fatigue, I have had my vision."

My paperback copy of Woolf's new, experimental non-linear novel that her Bloomsbury friends—artists, poets and intellectuals—dared and encouraged her to write is underlined, its margins crowded with my free-floating thoughts and feelings; awe at Woolf's insights into herself, human nature and Nature itself; her optimism that despite a World War that nearly wiped out a generation of young men and women, women who may not have died in trenches but drove trucks, bandaged wounds, knitted sweaters and kept families together—"set a table with flowers" and kept a national conversation alive with poetry, and their "special something"—empathy, truly knowing someone by their name. And mourned their fathers, husbands, brothers and sons. Lily Briscoe, who couldn't open herself to love, stands for all of us who fear commitment that exposes us to terrible sadness and anger that comes with loss. Minor characters, the poet, the housekeeper, the boy who rows the sailboat unto the rocky island where ships have foundered, and sailors drowned (elegant metaphors are old-school literature but forever new in Woolf's hands). Like Chaucer's Canterbury *Tales,* which begins in spring, a universal symbol of hope and renewal, we journey with them; it's the journey—not the destination that which is for all of us the same—that counts.

A question arises about the ending of this new form journey to a distant symbol of our need for security and constancy, bred into our DNA. Why does Lily need the perfectly drawn line to complete her canvas—which she accepts will molder in an attic, not at MOMA, the Met or Louvre, the Hermitage, or the British Museum? (I am not an admirer of Mondrian and his perfectly placed lines, but I do love his brilliant use of color.)

If this masterwork says anything, it says there is no perfection in art, literature, music, love, marriage—anything. Lily has no children and will never have the fecundity she envies in Mrs. Ramsay and the wisdom that comes with teaching children they can't have everything and life isn't fair, that marriage can never be perfectly fair—pretty mundane stuff—and that the perfect fruit on the perfectly set table will rot if not eaten or that a tornado can flatten a home in an instant. Jackson Pollack's drip paintings speak to modernity because they speak to process, mood, life as "the thing itself," shifting, not static—but flowing from the can as its nature permits—guided by an imperfect human hand. Perhaps Rembrandt, who hangs in every museum that can afford to have one, or Bruegel's view of life in its ugliness and stink, or Lucien Freud's portraits of naked bodies—none of them pretty, are all Modernists (as was Lucien's grandfather Sigmund).

Counterlives: An Homage
to *The Catcher in the Rye*: J.D. Salinger (1951) and *The Moviegoer*: Walker Percy (1961)

(With acknowledgement to *The Counterlife* by Philip Roth (1986)[17]

Preface

Dear Reader:

My decision to republish this essay, a version of which first appeared in *Hide and Seek/ Hidden and Found—In Search of a Balanced Life,* is due to my interest in two strong female characters: one a ten-year-old child, Phoebe (from *A Catcher on the Rye*), and the other a 30-year old emotionally disturbed woman (*The Moviegoer*). In the first publishing, my main focus was on two men in their lives: Holden Caulfield, 16 years old, and Binx Bolling, 30. This feels fresh to me and I hope it will to you.

In the preface to a short (unpublished) book I wrote in 2011, titled *How Can This Be? This Can't Be*

---

[17] Schwartz, Howard Lester, M.D. *Hide and Seek/Hidden and Found—In Search of a Balanced Life—Psychoanalytic Memoirs, Stories and Essays.* 2017, IPBooks, New York.

Me, I chose to explore developmental conflicts around love in the lives of three friends: Arnold, Samantha and Gordon. The title was meant to suggest that a main task of adolescence is the discovery and consolidation of a unique identity, a "me." While other tasks may be subsumed under this central task, this book reflected my personal and professional take on the matter. I believe that finding love and "falling in love is wonderful" and development is incomplete without this discovery.

There is much ugliness and many tragic aspects to life. Endings are not always happy, as the heroes in my books discover when they leave high school for the wider world. I chose to make my heroes healthy, privileged, well educated, creative, made of good stuff, with bright and loving caretakers. I also chose to create them as optimistic and hopeful, not cynical and alienated as some—too many—youths are today. I wanted them to pursue love in the wide, not exclusively sexual sense, and fulfill the dreams I envisioned for them. As Samantha, one of my characters, questioned: "Don't you wish it for me, too?"

Having followed all of my characters—Arnold, Gordon and Samantha, as well as Jared and Alice, and before them, Kenny and Benny—from fourth through 12th grade, I wanted to set them free to live on their own but wondered if I might want or need to return to their lives at some later time. It turned out I couldn't leave them alone very long, as I accidentally came upon two classic coming-of-age novels that forced me to reconsider my rather unrealistic, almost airbrushed "finding love" stories.

I came upon the books of Salinger and Percy in a stack in my son's study that he and my daughter-in-law had purchased for my grandson, Alexander, to get his personal library started. He was about to enter college at Tulane University, and had read Salinger in 12th grade but had not read Percy, whose National Book Award-winning novel is set in the Garden District culture of New Orleans, the place he would soon make his home.

It was shocking to me that I had never read *The Catcher in the Rye*, but not surprising that I had never heard of Walker Percy. My close reading of these books, twice no less, encouraged me to write this essay. I wondered if I might envision "counterlives" for my characters in the fashion of Philip Roth in his thoroughly modern 1986 novel *The Counterlife*, but decided I wasn't up to it. Salinger and Percy's sympathetically envisioned characters, classics in our American coming-of-age literature, have—better than I ever could—introduced us to the complexity, pitfalls, hard won victories and awful failures of young adulthood as their characters search for their authentic selves...unlike the airbrushed lives of Arnold, Samantha, Gordon and their friends.

Like my characters, Salinger's Holden Caulfield, age 16, and Percy's Binx (Jack) Bolling, age 30, come from privileged homes; but unlike my characters, they have experienced deaths, mental illness, failures in school, divorces, war and emotional abandonment. They are "searchers" in a world of adults who don't understand why they cannot settle for conventional success as measured by the lives of their parents and culture. In many ways, I now prefer these characters to my own.

Having read this far, I encourage you to put what is to follow aside and read these two marvelous books if you haven't already; or if you have, to read them again. Rejoin us when you're ready

Phoebe, *The Catcher in the Rye*

Imagined reader at my imagined literary soirée: *It's my pleasure to tell Phoebe's story because, of all the characters in these two books, she's, I mean I am, the best—smart, funny, lively, generous, and yes, intuitively wise beyond my years. I love my big brother and Holden loves me best, too. Of anyone, Holden visited me when he was depressed and suicidal. Holden's contemplating suicide was an escape from the fear of facing our parents yet again, even though he consciously denies feeling guilty or ashamed of failing out of his fourth private boarding school, losing, once again, contact with classmates who he derides as weird or phonies but actually are his only friends, having no back-up plan but to live alone in a cabin in the woods with no means of support except our parents, having used and even squandered all his savings on clubbing, alcohol and taxis, and now realizing he is homeless and may soon starve or freeze to death.*

Our younger brother Allie, whom Holden loved and respected for his intelligence and sweet nature, died of acute leukemia at age 11, four years or so before the events of The Catcher in the Rye, and Holden is still mourning him. A red hunting cap, the color of Allie's hair, which Holden impulsively bought for $1.00, knowing he has flunked out of Pencey, has warded off wind and rain on his lonely journey to Manhattan. Booze, jazz, and a failed encounter with a young prostitute who takes advantage of his vulnerability, could not save him. He has only me.

In what I perceive are the most brilliantly conceived moments of the story, Holden knocks on his parents' Manhattan apartment door, fearing to awaken them, but they are not home. Phoebe answers and sees Holden as the apparition he is, and in horror says, "You didn't get kicked out or anything, did you?... You did get kicked out! You did!... Oh, Holden!... Daddy'll kill you!"

Holden assures her their father won't kill him; he'll

get a ranch job in Colorado anyway. "The worst he'll do, he'll give me hell again, and then he'll send me to that goddam military school.... And in the first place, I won't even be around."

She confronts him, saying that he doesn't like anything or anybody, and he defends himself; but she is right. Then Holden says he likes Allie, "And I like what I'm doing right now. Sitting here talking with you, and talking, and thinking about stuff, and—" Then Phoebe, sounding frantic, says, "Allie's dead" and if somebody's dead and in Heaven, it's not as if it's something real. Holden replies, "Just because somebody's dead, you don't just stop liking them...especially if they were a thousand times nicer than people you know that're alive and all."

Their conversation goes on. Holden says he doesn't want to be a doctor, or a lawyer like his father and thinks to himself, "I'm not too sure old Phoebe knew what the hell I was talking about. I mean she's only a little child and all. But she was listening, at least. If somebody at least listens, it's not too bad."

Then he opens up to her.

> "I was thinking about something else—something crazy.... 'You know that song "If a body catch a body comin' through the rye!"? I'd like—'"

Phoebe, smart girl that she is, corrects him.

> "It's 'if a body meet a body coming through the rye'.... It's a poem. By Robert Burns.

>> "I thought it was 'If a bod catch a body,' I said. [A Freudian slip.] Anyway, I keep picturing all these little kids playing some game in this big

field of rye and all. Thousands of little kids and nobody's around—nobody big, I mean—except me. And I'm standing on the edge of some crazy cliff. What I have to do, I have to catch everybody if they start to go over the cliff—I mean if they're running and they don't look where they're going, I have to come out from somewhere and catch them. That's all I'd do all day. I'd just be the catcher in the rye and all. I know it's crazy but that's the only thing I'd really like to be. I know it's crazy."

Phoebe is silent and then says, "Daddy is going to kill you." Holden later dances with Phoebe. She can dance really well, as she gives herself up to dance in sync with her partner.

Recounting this scene, as told by my imagined narrator, I could barely catch my breath and my tears. All the searching, not understood nor genuinely listened to children are hurtling over a cliff, the cliff at which Holden stands struggling to resist his own suicidal impulse: one misstep and it's over. Where are the parents and well-meaning teachers and analysts? Phoebe intuitively knows he is at the edge of suicide and ironically warns him, "Daddy's going to kill you." Holden says, no he won't; he'll get sent to another school...but he won't go. Signal after signal indicate that he feels trapped and suicide is his way out. Allie is still loved but dead, so he gives his red hat, a talisman, to Phoebe; a prized possession now useless (another signal of the danger of imminent suicide). A failed attempt to use sex—a life force— has ended in humiliation (dancing with Phoebe is much better than sex with a stranger). Allie can't help him unless he joins—meets Holden— through death at the bottom of the cliff (more about Holden's struggle with religion appear later in the novel). But Phoebe, in the here and now, knows her brother needs her to want him to live and she will sacrifice her life for him.

Phoebe does not consciously recognize the irony in her warning, "Daddy'll kill you!" Where has Daddy been while tending to his career, rescuing clients and ignoring his children or his grieving wife who needs him to listen to her and share her grief? Is their father a workaholic who masks and avoids his own feelings? It is the grown-ups who aren't applying themselves to their jobs, so Holden has to function as the grown-up.

Phoebe returns the red hat to Holden because she knows he needs it (Allie) more than she does and offers to give up her comfortable life and her part in the upcoming school play that she wants her parents and Holden to attend. She will sacrifice it all to save Holden's life and live with him in his haven of choice in the woods. He is moved to tears by her love and decides not to run away but to accept analytic in-patient help rather than suicide or dropping out. The outcome for Holden is uncertain as it is for the lost, misunderstood child in all of us.

An aside to the reader:

Only in rewriting this essay do I more fully recognize my choice of Phoebe as a hero of modern literature. (There were other candidates, e.g., 13-year old Scout from *To Kill a Mockingbird*.) Salinger's more than "coming of age" novel is an example of the modernism which Virginia Woolf introduced to the world in 1927, as shocking and jarring to our senses as Jackson Pollock's drip paintings or Murasaki's audacious and hard to follow *Tale of Genji*, written a thousand years ago. Salinger incorporates psychotherapy—in- and out-patient—as Woolf introduces references to Freud and Horney and the crucial capacity of female empathy as a balance to men-from-Mars attitudes. Phoebe has ample empathy and compassion for her 16-year brother and will sacrifice her ambitions-—at least temporarily—to join him in self-imposed isolation so that he can write and heal himself. And she reads poetry—Robert Burns—central to her understanding of her brother's need to save children like him from committing suicide:

Comin thro' the Rye
by Robert Burns

Comin thro' the rye, poor body,
Comin thro' the rye,
She draigl't a' her petticoatie
Comin thro' the rye.

Oh Jenny's a' weet poor body
Jenny's seldom dry,
She draigl't a' her petticoatie
Comin thro' the rye.

Gin a body meet a body
Comin thro' the rye,
Gin a body kiss a body
Need a body cry.

Gin a body meet a body
Comin thro' the glen;
Gin a body kiss a body
Need the warld ken!

A close reading of Salinger, a well-read writer, will suggest similar themes in Woolf's adolescent characters, Cam and James, who band together to resist the tyranny of their father and don't want to be like him, just as neither Holden nor Binx (more later in this essay) want to be like theirs. Also similar are the themes of suicide (over a cliff or into the sea) and being rescued or becoming a hero—who "does but doesn't die." Binx just gets hung up on concertina fencing and is himself rescued, speaking to the complexity of life as it really is. (As told by Harold in the unedited version, worth reading). Binx marries Kate, who suffers from bi-polar disorder, but neither he nor Merle, her loyal psychiatrist, can rescue her and Kate, exhausted, succumbs to suicide, as does Mrs. Ramsay. (A biographical note: Virginia Woolf had a sound marriage with a man she loved and who loved and cared for as well as a man can, as she wrote to Leonard in her suicide note. But when she could no longer bear being a burden to him or her own pain, she loaded rocks in her trousers and drowned in the sea.)

Written March 28, 1941, from Wikidata:

Dearest,

I feel certain that I am going mad again. I feel we can't go through another of those terrible times. And I shan't recover this time. I begin to hear voices, and I can't concentrate. So, I am doing what seems the best thing to do. You have given me the greatest possible happiness. You have been in every way all that anyone could be. I don't think two people could have been happier 'til this terrible disease came. I can't fight any longer. I know that I am spoiling your life, that without me you could work. And you will I know. You see I can't even write this properly. I can't read. What I want to say is I owe all the happiness of my life to you. You have been entirely patient with me and incredibly good. I want to say that — everybody knows it. If anybody could have saved me it would have been you. Everything has gone from me but the certainty of your goodness. I can't go on spoiling your life any longer.

I don't think two people could have been happier

than we have been. V.

Again, to the reader:

The original essay in *Hide and Seek* is quite long and as my interest is in Phoebe and Kate, I will take the liberty to edit it to emphasize their different characters and ways in which I see them as heroes.

Edited excerpts:

From the introduction:

Strangely, I hesitate to begin writing because I am not interested in a compare and contrast review of two books. Were it possible, I would sit us around a conference table or better yet my living room, with drinks and snacks, and just talk about them. My hesitation has suggested a way to create such an environment, so bear with me. Let's pretend our group of readers has people with the same names as characters in these novels and speaks from their namesakes' points of view. This contrivance might be fun if we can ignore the fact that I am actually playing all the characters myself. Yet isn't that what writers and dreamers always do? We must assume the narrators have read both books, know the back- stories of the book in which they do not appear and are willing to join the game.

Kate: *Binx, like me is "searching" and so is Holden. Binx is searching for the father he doesn't know, always questioning his father's sister, Aunt Emily, and his mother who divorced his father and remarried a very different man—she is no longer a prominent surgeon's wife but a happy redneck living with a passel of kids in a bayou rather than in the Garden District.*

Binx knows who others expect him to be but, like Holden, he cannot genuinely apply himself to their goals. He drifts and searches and daydreams in his more real world of movies. Should he become a prominent stockbroker like his Uncle, or a practicing physician with golden hands like his unhappy father who fell into a serious depression because he wasn't a researcher? His Aunt Emily keeps telling him he is cut out to be a researcher, but he knows she is dreaming and seeing him as his father. She doesn't get who he is. He joins the correct fraternity at Tulane, but daydreams for four years as a disinterested student without goals. He is not overtly depressed like his beautiful cousin Kate, nor does he become deeply depressed like his father because merely practicing surgery is not enough for someone who longs to do basic research to find a cure for cancer and save the world. According to Binx's mother, his father lost his appetite for life and wouldn't eat unless she read to him, a kind of moviegoer like his son. WWII broke out and provided his father with a purpose for living. He regained the 30 pounds he'd lost and promptly enlisted in the U.S. Army Air Force,—serving as a pilot, not a physician—and died an ordinary death in a crash, unlike the heroic death he may have sought.

Kate is lost and searching for sanity, a human presence to hold her and recognize that her charm and cleverness is a defense against her suicidal urges to escape the pain of making decisions about the simplest things, such as how to take a trolley car or talk to a stranger. Her psychiatrist, Merle, is reliable, available to see her in his office regularly— forever if necessary—to pump her stomach in an emergency room when she overdoses on barbiturates and to trust her will to survive by not hospitalizing her. But she knows she has to free herself from him. She decides to live—not as the bi-polar child she was before surviving the death of her fiancé in a car accident, suffering with survivor guilt as well as her pre-existing chronic depression—but as an adult, risking yet again a commitment to marriage.

Kate understands that Binx uses movies to make himself feel real, part of a place with real smells and real people, because she too does not feel real. She loves the transient freedom of riding a train somewhere as a watcher of outside real places, but fears arriving as a tourist and actually living there. Chicago is too far from New Orleans, but even New Orleans, with the allure of Mardi Gras, isn't safe. She needs to be rescued and Binx, her cousin, is willing to marry her, sacrificing his ambitions to become a wealthy real estate developer or even to own a garage (anything but a doctor or big-time investment broker). He has no interest in medicine or medical research because it means applying himself. Only movies, transient relationships with his pretty secretaries, small town suburban life, solitary daybreak walks on empty streets while planning his next trip to see a movie in a distant town or at an old familiar Tulane neighborhood theater where he drifted through school daydreaming and partying with pretty girls (and fraternity boys who partied too, but aimed high) make his life tolerable. After a last fling at Mardi Gras with a barely functioning suicidal Kate, Binx capitulates to accepting an arranged entry to medical school—never mentioned but most certainly Tulane—and life as Kate's caretaker. He at least will have a purpose in life; perhaps even a heroic purpose in doing for her what he needs for himself. Life is not a movie that you can walk out of. Is it sad or inevitable that Binx can't forever live as a lost boy searching for a father in the Garden District and a mother with a passel of half-siblings in the Lafitte bayou, going to Church on Sunday and pretending to pray to a God in which he doesn't believe?

Skipping ahead now for Binx's Aunt Emily's take on Binx and Kate:

Aunt Emily: *It's complicated for Binx. He's a man of the South and knows our manners, rituals and the* importance we place on civility and appearances. Having responsibility requires respecting these traditions, but he doesn't feel them as genuinely his traditions. He wouldn't miss Mardi Gras but also won't accept an invitation to join a krewe as a pillar of the business community. Living in Gentilly and having small-town clients and a quiet life suits him fine.

It's not that he isn't ambitious or doesn't value money. He wants to develop some real estate he inherited, swamp land really, and have a comfortable life, just not that much. Maybe it's because his father married beneath his class and wasn't happy working as a practicing surgeon, but after their divorce, his mother married a redneck from bayou land, lives near a swamp, fishes for her family's breakfast, goes to church on Sunday and was happy. Like his father, he has fun with his secretaries but unlike him, won't marry one. He and Kate would make a perfect couple and he could settle her down, move downtown, eat oysters on Magazine Street, work as a broker and have a good life. He just isn't interested. He distracts himself from feeling depressed with his magic red MG two-seater to impress girls he wants to seduce, knowing the car and the pretty woman of the moment will soon lose their power and what will he then have—movies?

It's curious that Holden's magic talisman is a ridiculous looking red hunting cap with earflaps. Holden offers it to Phoebe because he loves her and as he intends to self-destruct one way or another, it is no longer of use to him but may be of use to her. We are left to wonder about the over-determined symbolic meanings of red as a magic life-saving talisman, or a stop sign warning us that danger lies ahead and we should change course, or as a symbol of wished for strength and virility (Binx), and at root, a link to red-haired Allie who Holden could not save and now cannot save himself. To save a child or anyone from cancer *or devote one's life to cancer research appears as the highest goal of Binx's father and the one that Binx rejects because he knows it isn't in him—nor was it in his father. It is terribly sad that Holden and Binx must turn to symbols or children or Kate, a child-like woman, for love or any hope of life and happiness or salvation if one believes salvation is possible. Phoebe loves purely as does Lonnie (Binx's half-brother by his mother's second marriage). Kate trusts that she can allow herself to love Binx if he will care for her and never expect more than she can give. Love and self-sacrifice are linked in these dyadic relationships, suggesting the earliest roots of maternal love and religious beliefs.*

(No one is named Binx, but Jack is Binx's middle name):

Jack, on searching: *To search is to have an identity, and not to be searching is to cease to exist. I am searching for my father, love and life itself.*

Kate: *I know our time is nearly up. This has been a long discussion, more like a triple overtime session, but I'm pleased to have the last word. I think our narrator has put a lot of himself into writing about us and I think he's "got it," but if he hasn't got it all, at least he's got us thinking about serious matters that will always be relevant. I think he's had fun writing this essay, which you know was done in Mexico where he vacations every winter. He must identify with Sam Yeager, his unnamed proxy, just like Binx does. Holden at age 16 is still seeking his muse and his Moleskin journal, but in reading this book, we know he has found it.*

Because Kate has a chronic biologic emotional disorder, she will always need support and medication—and perhaps periodic hospitalization—and Merle will be able to fulfill that role for her. Most analysts today would be cautious about deep, exploratory psychoanalytic therapy with someone as fragile as Kate. But she is not just a diagnosis. She is a damaged soul that needs to heal, which for her will be a life-long process. She needs to trust that love need not end in tragedy. She needs a willing everyday partner who can empathize with her and allow her to help him. She needs Binx and he needs her. Analysts, the best of them, can't cure and sometimes life can't cure. I hope those who have been encouraged to read these books will wonder what life holds for Holden and Binx, Kate and Phoebe; at least think of them now and then. (Our analyst author has "evolved" since writing How Can This Be? This Can't Be Me *in 2011 and intends these novels to be read as "counter-lives" for his too comfortably privileged characters.)*

After completing this essay from a psychoanalytic perspective, I did some research—not too much and mostly out of curiosity—as to literary takes on these coming-of-age classics. They both have been much reviewed, but I got lucky and discovered an essay in *The Atlantic*[18] in which Andrew Santella writes of his obsession with *The Moviegoer*, a book he first read as a sophomore in college and has read yearly in the days preceding Mardi Gras ever since. You will be doing yourself a favor if you read it too, as kind of a rich dessert after a hearty meal. (You may feel my meal is barely digestible although I took great pains in preparing it.) Percy does not tell us what life holds in store for Binx and Kate, but another author did—a teaser to get you to eat dessert.

Santella writes:

> "In the years since I first read *The Moviegoer*, I married, became a father, and learned some of the tricks we all learn for passing as an adult in an adult world. But reading *The Moviegoer* annually

---

[18] "My Childish. Unhealthy, Joyous Obsession with *The Moviegoer*." *The Atlantic*, March 7, 2014.

has given me an excuse to stay in contact with my 20-year-old self. Going back to Binx's New Orleans every year is, in fact, a little like going to a reunion: Binx and Kate and the various versions of me all getting together to check each other out and see who has thrived and who looks really bad.

"One of the things I looked for in *The Moviegoer* year after year was some clue to what happened to Binx and Kate. The novel ends ambiguously. Binx and Kate are supposed to marry and Binx is supposed to go to medical school. The plan is for them to live a good, simple life, to 'walk abroad on a summer night...and see a show and eat some oysters down on Magazine.'

"But what really happens? I finally got an answer, not from *The Moviegoer* but from another very good New Orleans novel, John Gregory Brown's *Decorations in a Ruined Cemetery*, from 1994. I'd already been rereading *The Moviegoer* for more than a decade when I got to Brown's book. And just as I was coming to the conclusion of Brown's novel, I got to a passage that just about knocked me out of my chair. A stockbroker-turned-doctor named Jack makes an appearance. Some things about Jack seem awfully familiar. Jack likes to go to the movies. Like Binx, he drives a tiny red sports car. Like Binx, he's a Korean War veteran who once lived in Gentilly. And did I mention that Jack is Binx's real name?... It's Binx, of course, making a cameo appearance in Brown's novel. But there's one more thing about Jack that made me sure of his identity. Brown writes that he 'had been married, but his wife had killed herself some years before.' I'm not sure I've ever been quite as stunned by a single sentence in a novel as I was by that one. It was like being surprised by the news of a friend's sudden death. Except...I should have seen it coming all the way.

"That revelation changed the way I read *The Moviegoer*. Now, I'm not quite as attracted to Binx's wit, to his charm, to his antic detachment. Now when I read *The Moviegoer*, I mostly notice the psychic danger just beneath the surface. It's a strange thing to mourn the loss of a character in a novel. It's even stranger to identify so strongly with a character that you almost feel complicit in the story's unhappy ending. But I've crawled so deep into *The Moviegoer* over the years that it's hard to tell where I start and where the novel begins.... If you spend enough time with a book over enough years, you may start to think it belongs to you somehow. But what if it's really the other way around."

Yes, as "Kate" says...I've evolved since writing *How Can This Be? This Can't Be Me*, and I do intend these novels to be read as "counter-lives" for my—perhaps unrealistically—too comfortably privileged characters. Thank you for accepting my suggestion that you read these classics of American literature and for participating with me as imagined live participants in discussing them. I am old-fashioned and prefer the written word to video-conferencing on Skype or FaceTime, which, in any event would be impossible for the task have I set here for myself.

Modernism—the Legacy of Virginia Woolf
Lives in the Voice of Lauren Groff

Once again following my story—heroic women in literature—where it leads, I arrive at a genius whose non-linear short stories are strung together—or so it seems to me—as though they were conceived as a novel, like Woolf's daring story of the Ramsays, their children, "the mystery of the thing that bonded them" and the undertones of death and despair, with glimmers of hope: the Lighthouse (where a solitary keeper lives with his tubercular son). Although I thought I would discuss Groff's best-selling literary novel *Fates and Furies* and then move on to *Florida*,[19] I realized that, while I admired the novel, I didn't like the people, and found the plot too neat and contrived...apparently not the case with reviewers, nor with President Obama, who praised it.

Florida has been widely reviewed, but although I have said I value introductions, I have read none. The book is organized into 11 chapters, a half dozen or so of which I read on my Kindle (and then bought the book because it is easier to underline as I read), with mounting discomfort and fascination, like a horror movie you can't take your eyes off or Tolstoy's short novella *The Death of Ivan Ilyich* (1886). My plan is to read and comment on each chapter, so I hope you, dear reader, will bear with me and see this book to its conclusion.

Ch.1: Ghosts and Empties

"I have somehow become a women who yells," writes Groff, "and because I do not want to be a woman who yells, whose little children walk around with frozen,

---

[19] Groff, Lauren. *Florida*. New York: Riverhead Books, 2018.

watchful faces, I have taken to lacing my running shoes after dinner and going out into the twilit streets for a long walk, leaving the undressing and sluicing and reading and singing and tucking in of the boys to my husband, a man who does not yell."

As she runs in the cold night air, "feral cats dart underfoot, bird-of-paradise flowers poke out of their shadows, smells are exhaled into the air: oak dust, slime mold, camphor." In this neighborhood of historic, rotting Victorian homes once left to squatters and the poor, a 50-year old woman jogger was once dragged into the azalea bushes and raped, a pack of pit bulls recently mauled a mother and baby. We learn that the protagonist moved here a decade ago because the real estate was cheap, because "if I had to live in the South, with its boiled peanuts and Spanish moss dangling like armpit hair, at least I wouldn't barricade myself with my whiteness in a gated community," but the neighborhood is now "infected" with middle-class gentrification.

On her night walks, she observes the remnants of her neighbors' messy lives: one January, "I watched a Christmas bouquet of roses on one mantel diminish until the flowers were a blighted shrivel and the water a green scum," and she passes a convent that once held six nuns, now reduced to three old ladies "squeaking around that immense space in their sensible shoes" whom she imagines as surviving nuclear holocaust in the backyard bomb shelter, singing and praying, "while, aboveground, all has been blasted black, and rusted hinges rasp the wind."

On her way home, she passes friends and stranger, including an elegant tall woman, seemingly in pain and perhaps dying, as she walks her Great Dane...a homeless lady "emitting a...feminine stink"...the therapist sitting alone at his desk who had sex with the wife of a patient who later murdered her during coitus, but merely wounded the therapist, now an alcoholic.

When she returns home, "It's too much, it's too much, I shout at my husband...and he looks at me, afraid, this giant gentle man...and says, softly, I don't think you've walked it off yet," and sends her back out into the darkened, more dangerous streets.

At home she reads about the disasters of the world, glaciers dying like living people, an otter eating two cygnets whose two siblings die of heart failure and whose parents (black swans) go into mourning...she sees her husband, who has left his computer open, a conversation and a flash of bare flesh she was not meant to see....

And then when she can bear no more...a young fat boy she has seen at night running on his treadmill has become slim and handsome, assuring her that "not everything is decaying faster than we can love it"...and the black swans at the duck pond are building a new nest...and there's "a pleasant smell like campfires in the air"...and she returns home to kiss her sleeping children and assure them that "I have not been gone, that my spirit, hours ago, slipped back into the house" to kiss "this gentle man whom I love so desperately...and curled myself on the pillows to breathe into me the breath that my children breathed out." She notes that "Soon, tomorrow the boys will be men, then the men will leave the house, and my husband and I will look at each other, crouching under the weight of all that we wouldn't or couldn't yell, as well as those all those hours outside walking together, my body, my shadow and the moon." And the moon is laughing...but not at us, "we lonely humans, who are far too small, and our lives too fleeting to give us any notice at all."

Groff is hopeful that life offers us opportunities to live better in ways we can control because there is so much we cannot control: the ugliness, stink, decay, all listed by her (I almost typed Woolf) like the horrors in a modern Brueghel painting. We can love and forgive those who disappoint us. Mrs. Ramsay forgives Mr. Ramsay because he demands it, and she knows he needs sympathy; and the narrator/author (Groff?) kisses her gentle giant who has cared for their children but spent time online doing what she didn't want to see or think about. Maybe all mothers want their children to feel secure: to share their bodies and breaths with them, feel their warmth and inhale their youth, only to know, if they do their job well, that they will leave but want to return as adults with their children (to "grandma's house"). But what if those children don't return? What if women and men are not friends and lovers "till death do them part" if they are lonely humans living only to await death? With no one to call or visit or help them as they age, who will remember them (us)? And if they have no memories of shared walks in the night under the light of a moon, how sad and pitiable they (we) all are.

I don't expect happy endings, but let's read on.

Ch. 2: At the Round Earth's Imagined Corners

The chapter title suggests and invites us to imagine a story at the corners of the earth, a strange and ominous place.

> "Jude was born in a Cracker-style house at the edge of a swamp that boiled with unnamed species of reptiles.... Air conditioning was for the rich.... Jude's father was a herpetologist at the university, and if snakes hadn't slipped their way into their hot house, his father would have filled it with them anyway. Coils of rattlers sat in formaldehyde on the windowsills. Writhing knots

of reptiles lived in the coop out back.... At an early age, Jude learned to keep a calm heart when touching fanged things. He was barely walking when his mother came into the kitchen to find a coral snake chasing its red and yellow tail around his wrist [they're poisonous]. His father was watching from across the room, laughing. His mother was Yankee, a Presbyterian. She was... afraid of scaly creatures, and sang hymns in an attempt to keep them out. When she was pregnant with Jude's sister, she came into the bathroom to take a cool bath one August night and, without her glasses, missed a three-foot albino alligator her husband had stored in the bathtub. The next morning, she was gone. She returned a week later. And after Jude's sister was born dead, his mother never stopped singing under her breath."

Early in my psychiatric training (1964–1967), I was introduced to *I Never Promised You a Rose Garden* (1964), a semi-autobiographical novel written by Joanne Greenberg under the penname Hannah Green. It describes her in-patient treatment with a talented psychoanalyst who listened carefully to her "imagined corner" of the world as part of what was then a novel form of treatment for schizophrenia, but later reevaluated as an actually non-malignant psychotic illness. Greenberg's analyst, Frieda Fromm-Reichmann (a German psychiatrist and contemporary of Sigmund Freud who immigrated to America during World War II) empathically warned her that the talking cure was hard but "I never promised you a rose garden." So, it is with Lauren Groff who in her opening pages of this chapter may be warning us that Jude's life (Jude is the Hellenized version of the Hebrew name Judah, meaning to praise) is to be praised (speculative; maybe she just liked the name). If so, praised for what?

Jude is a man with a sadistic father who grudgingly recognizes his son's genius at math but who will only relate to him if he hunts snakes with him; a man with a mentally ill mother who dies of cancer at a young age; a man who survives a life-threatening accident and is rescued by an overweight caretaker he feels obligated to marry; a man who is never able to feel comfortable around people and retains a lifelong terror of alligators and hatred of his father (who dies and rots alone after being bitten by a snake). Jude goes deaf and can't be cured, feeling even more alone because he can't hear his family at a Thanksgiving dinner. Seeking solace, he goes out in the jolly boat (flat bottomed fishing boat) where he is becalmed and, near death from sunburn and dehydration, dreams of his father and thinks, "I'm not like you, Dad…. I don't prefer snakes to people." When the breeze picks up and Jude drifts toward shore, he is again rescued by his wife (into whose neck he can snuggle as he did with his mother as a boy); and he allows himself to think, "You were a nasty, unhappy man. And I always hated you."

Yes, Jude is a survivor who is to be pitied and praised.

Ch. 3: Dogs Go Wolf

Once again, the title suggests danger and loneliness, as in the common expression "lone wolf" or "loner." The evolution of the dogs we know as pets as well as working dogs of all sizes and breeds were once wolves, hunters that depended on the unity of the pack to survive, from Alpha wolves, the CEOs, to Beta, the strongest and females, to scouts, each with their evolved (in the DNA) capacities. When a wolf no longer serves the pack, he is expelled from the family and left to howl alone in the wilderness, where he cannot survive: an orphan looking for a foster family to adopt him. (I relied on the well-researched novel by Jodi Picoult of a father who leaves his children to live alone in a wilderness until he is accepted as a wolf, allowed into a pack and learns their ways; only then can he return to his abandoned children, hoping to be accepted by them; a reversal of Groff's story.[20]) As if to emphasize the dehumanizing effect of abandonment and the forced regression to basic needs for food, shelter, clean water, clothing and stories as substitutes for what they need to survive—hope above all—the characters are not named; they could be any of us and have been all of us. The story begins:

> "The storm came and erased the quiet. Well, the older sister thought, an island is never really quiet. Even without the storm, there were waves and wind and air conditioners and generators and animals moving out there in the dark.
>
> "What the storm had erased was the silence from the other cabin. For hours, there had been no laughing, no bottle caps falling, none of the bickering that the girls had become used to over the past two days.
>
> "This was because there were no more adults. They had been left alone on the island, the two little girls. Four and seven. Pretty little things, strangers called them.... Hoochies in waiting, their mother joked, but she watched them anxiously from the corner of her eye. She was a good mother.
>
> "The fluffy white dog had at least stopped his yowling. He had crept close to the girls' bed, but when they tried to stroke him, he snapped

---

[20] Picoult, Jodi, *Lone Wolf*. New York, Atria Books, 2012.

at their hands. The animal was torn between his hatred of children and his hatred of the wild storm outside.

"The big sister said, Once upon a time, there was a—

"—princess, the little sister said.

"Rabbit, the big sister said.

"—Rabbit princess, the little sister said.

"Once upon a time, there was a tiny purple rabbit, the older sister said. A man scooped her up in his net. Her family tried to stop him, but they couldn't. The man went into the city and took the rabbit to a pet store.... All day long people stuck their hands in to touch the purple rabbit. Finally a girl bought her and brought her home. It was better there, but the rabbit missed her family. She grew and slept with the girl in her bed, but most days she stared out the window all sad."

And from this introduction the story becomes almost unbearable to read. After all, Groff "never promised us a rose garden." There is no escape from the mendacity and treachery of the adults who hedonistically seek only their own pleasure. There is no escape from the island except for the dog that runs away, hides in a cave and only when desperate for water, comes back, and then abandons the children he hates. He is too mean to die and will live on the island alone forever; a fate we readers know is wished for by the girls as just punishment in- kind for all adults. They hallucinate about the food and water they don't have tell stories about growing enormously fat, devouring people, eating them alive to their bones and blood, and escaping death by floating away on the clouds above. When a man arrives by boat, the big sister knows he is bad—a repeat of the purple rabbit kidnapper—and she knows enough to warn her little sister to be quiet and hide until he leaves. The girls learn survival techniques that depend on them working together, hauling water from a polluted pond and boiling it before drinking.

Spoiler alert; they are rescued by a man and fat woman (fat as a symbol of the possibility of capacity to share generously). But I won't give it all away.

Also, as I write, I'm reconsidering my notion that the author conceived of these stories as a non-linear novel. She published them in magazines, as 20 to 40 page stories, about all that a reader could bear in one dose. But let's read on.

Ch. 4: The Midnight Zone

"It was an old hunting camp shipwrecked in twenty miles of scrub. Our friend had seen a Florida panther sliding through the trees there a few days earlier.... my small boys...had wanted hermit crabs, wakeboards and sand for spring break. Instead they got ancient sinkholes filled with ferns, potential death by cat.... If anyone died it was going to be us, our skulls popping in the jaws of an endangered cat. It turned out to be a bad joke, because someone actually had died, that morning, in one of my husband's apartment buildings. A fifth-floor occupant had killed herself....

"For years at a time, I was good only at the things that interested me, and since all that interested me was my books and my children, the rest of life had sort of inched away.... And while it's true that my children were endlessly fascinating…being a mother never had been, and all that seemed assigned by default of gender I would not do because it felt insulting. I would not buy clothes, I would not make dinner, I would not keep schedules, I would not make playdates, never ever. Motherhood meant, for me, that I would take the boys on monthlong adventures to Europe, teach them to blast off rockets, to swim for glory. I taught them how to read, but they could make their own lunches…. My husband had to be the one to make up for the depths of my lack. It is exhausting living in debt that increases every day but that you have no intention of repaying.

"Two days, he promised. Two days and he'd be back…. He bent to kiss me, but I gave him my cheek and rolled over…."

She overfeeds her boys to keep them quiet and worries about the panther. Then she has an accident while standing on a revolving stool to change a light bulb; she falls and suffers a concussion and a lacerated scalp. Her frightened children, especially the little one, feed and bandage her, give her milk and water, clean up her vomit and read to her to keep her from falling into a coma. Her smaller boy cries, "But what if she's all a sudden dead and I'm all a sudden alone?" She too cries as she calls her older boy Sweetness because she can't remember his name. She won't allow him to try to walk 20 miles to town to get help because "there was a panther between us and there, but also possibly terrible men, sinkholes, alligators, the end of the world." The boys sing to her and tell her about a fish called *the humuhumunukunukuāpua'a*, "over and over, laughing, to the tune of 'Twinkle, Twinkle, Little Star.' They told

WOMEN: BIOLOGY, CULTURE AND LITERATURE

me about...the World Pool, in which one current goes one way, another goes another way, and where they meet to make a tornado of air, which stretches...from the midnight zone, where the fish are blind, all the way up to the birds." She experiences depersonalization—an out of body experience—on the way to recovery and a deep empathic bond for her children. When her husband returns, she read in his face "fear, and it was vast, it was elemental, like the wind itself...."

Just to get it off my chest...I'd like to know the names of these children who teach their mother to be the mother that they need, and I don't understand why Groff doesn't tell us. I speculated about this in the last story too, and in this story it may again be a way to show us through repetition that you can love without intimacy until, when your defenses are down, you can utter a name, "Sweetness." Life can be sweet if only *she*—the mother—can stop obsessing about the dangers of sinkholes, alligators and bad men, and enjoy the beauty of her children's laughter, their funny words and the wonder of their bodies pressed against hers (us, our mothers). What is her husband so afraid of? She knows she is dying. Her little boy fears it too. So many ways we can die: suicide, panthers, falls...but the word we all dread and is not named, cancer—is the stalker from within.

Ch. 5: Eyewall

This story feels very personal to me as I experienced the aftermath of Hurricane Katrina (August 23, 2005), which hit Mississippi where my son, daughter-in-law and eight-year-old grandson were living. My grandson's second-grade classroom and all the schools were closed. There were downed trees and tarps on roofs everywhere. His parents wanted him out of there as soon as possible, not just for his safety, but in fear of a weakened tree falling on their home or on their car.

My son, a physician, had to attend his patients and take his share of hospital duty, including calling around to find a roofer (they were in short supply as nothing interferes with hunting season in Mississippi, except for essential services, e.g., police, fire departments, rescue squads and medicine). If the roof was covered, repairs could wait; insurance adjusters had to first assess the damage anyway. The airports were open and guarded by men in khakis carrying submachine guns. Wind and heavy rain was the enemy, not people traumatized by loss of their homes, property or the lives of family and friends. My family lived in a single-story ranch house on a two-mile long and mile-wide lake. A thick tree limb was shorn from its trunk, and as though it was a javelin hurled by Goliath, pierced a picture window facing the lake and the heart of a girl (I'm not sure, but I think it was a schoolmate of my grandson). People in Mississippi board up their windows or have special storm doors, but even if the window had been boarded, it might not have stopped Goliath's javelin.

I flew to New Orleans and brought my grandson home with me, where we played endless card games and I read to him. When his parents asked for his return after his school reopened about ten days later, my wife flew with him into Jackson, where his parents picked him up. When we next visited Mississippi, many blue tarps were still up, but the New Orleans airport was no longer patrolled by armed men. There were fewer travelers and some stores had gone out of business. The Lake Pontchartrain Causeway was reduced to one lane and reconstruction had begun.

My grandson does not appear to have been

traumatized, but he doesn't tell me his dreams. I proposed a camping and rafting trip on the Yampa River, the last undammed river draining into the Colorado. We had a great adventure and never talked about Katrina or the uprooted trees, blue tarps and sudden death of a little girl by a spear thrown by Goliath.

Pictures do not always speak louder than a thousand words, especially in the voice of Lauren Groff:

> "It began with the chickens. They were Rhode Island Reds and I'd raised them from chicks. Though I called until my voice gave out, they'd huddled in the darkness under the house, a dim mass faintly pulsing. Fine, you ungrateful turds! I'd said before abandoning them to the storm. I stood in the kitchen at the one window I'd left unboarded and watched the hurricane's bruise spreading in the west. I felt the chickens' fear rising through the floorboards to pass through me like prayers....

> "All the other creatures of the earth flattened themselves, dug in. I stood in my window watching, a captain at the wheel, as the first

gust filled the oaks on the other side of the lake.... It shivered my lawn, my garden, sent the unplucked zucchini swinging like church bells. And then the wind smacked the house. Bring it on! I shouted. Or, maybe this is another thing in my absurd life that I whispered."

And then, "My best laying hen was scraped from under the house and slid in a horrifying diagonal across the window" and was blown away.

Her late husband makes an appearance, a poet older than she by 30 years, with brown eyes that bored through her, that made her fall for him. But a week after he leaves her, he dies in the arms of a girl "so preposterously young that I assumed they conversed in baby talk."

"He hadn't wanted children until he ended up fucking one.... He came closer and stood next to me. I went very still, as I always did near him.... "You're still here, of course, he said. Even though they told you to get out days ago.

"This house is old, I said, It has lived through other storms.

"You never listen to anyone he said.... He drank a swig of wine and moaned in appreciation.... And then it was only the storm and the house and me."

Who will appear next, ghosts from her past? You can count on it, because now the *unnamed* woman is into the surreal as a means of examining her responsibility for being alone, aging and drinking too much. She can't dig herself into the mud, like a baby alligator, to hide from her choices; she has to own up to them. But we might think, *haven't we fallen in love, passionately in love, for a beautiful other, an exciting other, but sensed we should not follow wherever they lead, backed away and then dashed forward, fearing to lose 'that thing we feel'*? (Orpheus and Eurydice /Anna and Vronsky/ Mrs. Ramsay and her husband who oozes asperity and narcissism but needs to be remembered as a man who made it to the Lighthouse and led the Charge of the Light Brigade. See Tolstoy and Woolf essays. The Myth of Orpheus and Eurydice, which I have written about in *Hide and Seek/Hidden and Found (2017)* is a tale of infidelity that challenges the concept of basic trust between lovers.)

> "From behind the flattened blueberries, a nightmare creature of mud stood and leaned against the wind. It showed itself to be a man only moments before the wind picked up and slammed him into the door.... The man crawled and helped me push the door until at last it closed....
>
> "The man was mudstruck, naked and laughing.... I saw that he was my old college boyfriend.... Oh! he shouted when he could speak. He'd always been a cheery boy, talkative and loving. He clutched my face between his hands, and said, You're old! You should wear the bottom of your trousers rolled....

He had committed suicide, she learned second- or third-hand, in a cheap motel in Canada, but she barely believed the story.

> "It's so strange, I said. You were always the happiest person I knew. You were so happy I had to break up with you."

In their youth, he had become an alcoholic and she had tired of his neediness, his late-night phone calls. She had sold one of her ovaries to pay for a trip to Spain and lost him in Barcelona; when she found him, she realized that what thought was a rose tattoo behind his ear was a bullet hole he'd earned in a duel.

> "My God, I loved you, I said. I had played it close to my chest then; I had thought not telling him was the source of my power over him."

They had nine imaginary children, all prodigies with classical names like Cleanth and Clothilde, "with your brains and <u>my</u> looks."

> "He lifted the back of my hand and kissed it. It's too bad, he murmured.... I saw my beautiful boy swan-dive into the three-foot-deep pond that had been m yard.... Then he imitated one of my dead chickens floating about in the water, her two wings cocked skyward.... Like synchronized swimmers, they swirled about each other, arms to the sky, and then, in a gulp, both sank."

She drinks more wine (too much), the water continues to rise, and the wild rats and raccoons try to escape to the upper floors of the house. Cooling herself in a tub in the bathroom, the storm lifts off the roof and she wonders how it all will end, as a water moccasin crawls up the pipes and rests between her thighs. And now comes the last ghost from her past:

> "[The light goes out.] There rose in its place there rose the sweet smell of pipe smoke.
>
> "Jesus Christ, I said.
>
> "No. It's your father....Watch your language my love."

Her father sits near her, and she touches his hand, "feeling the sop of his flesh against the fragile bone....

eaten from the inside by cancer" (There, the word is finally said out loud.) Her mother, an alcoholic, hadn't told her, sent her away to Girl Scout Camp. While he hallucinated about his Hungarian village with cherry trees and bellowing bulls in rut, she stole a sailboat and hallucinated about her childhood home.

Now, as her father's ghost sits holding her hand over the edge of the tub, "He smoked, I drank, and the world tired itself out with its tantrum." She remembers how angry and lonely she became when he spoke Hungarian to his parents and shut her out. She tells him, "I hated that you opened your mouth and suddenly became another person." (I am the child of two Hungarian parents and know exactly how she felt.)

"You'll be A-OK, he said.

"That's no wisdom coming from you, I said. Everything's all right for the dead."

The storm has stripped the house of its window frames and many of her belongings. "My life was scattered into three counties. Someone found a novel with my bookplate in it sunning itself on top of a car in Georgia. Everywhere I looked, the dead." Children drowned, old friends carried off, entire fields ruined. "My chickens... blown apart, their feathers freckling the ground. For weeks, the stench of their rot would fill my dreams."

But spring and hope return to a cleansed world.

"And there I stopped, breathless. I laughed. Isn't this the fucking kicker, I said aloud. Or maybe I didn't.

"Houses contain us; who can say what we contain? Out where the steps had been, balanced beside the drop-off; one egg, whole, and mute, holding all the light of dawn in its skin."

I hesitate to comment on this mysterious metaphor which left me as breathless as the author who wrote it; a *Woolfian* new form of modernism

Ch. 6: For the God of Love, For the Love of God and Ch. 7: Salvador

Two stories, bookended, speak to the dangers and allure of life in all its complexity. No longer are snakes, alligators, panthers and sinkholes to be feared, but only our passions and their consequences, our inner life. Nature takes on a symbolic meaning in both, as it does in the previous stories (swamps, winds that becalm and suddenly pick up to move us to a safe shore); but especially more so in these two stories. I don't know when Groff wrote them, but placing them back to back speaks to the push-pull of forces, the childhood sexuality of Leo, a four-year-old boy who feels erotic oedipal love, murderous rage at being abandoned, the sublime pleasure of being bathed by a young woman (Mina, his cousin, whose mother has not spoken to her in three years and who gave her up to be raised by her older sister Amanda), who sings to him as song birds and raptors fall from the sky—a bad omen we are told—and stink when you immolate their corpses, and the unbridled pleasure of riding a carousel and choosing a monkey over all the horses. And the burden of knowing what the adults are up to, seeing, sensing and remembering all, as we have been told to do again and again—everything.

It is unmistakable that the author cares deeply about children and holds a mirror to us, we who betray them through our hedonism, through not understanding what they like and don't like—buying them macaroons that they hate and then hide in a chimney for the birds to eat because they can't tell us and hurt our feelings...we who can't see that they hate us and would kill us if they could.

After using detailed quotes from the text of chapters 1–5, I decided to write this chapter from a distance, as though I were just telling you what these stories are about, what I loved and didn't, what excited me, appalled, saddened and frightened me (I couldn't find humor anywhere)...as though we were talking in a book club or seminar or as if I were writing a review. I am purposely not going back to my notes.

In no particular order:

(Ch. 6:) I loved that Mina after completing her junior year at college comes to stay with Amanda and realizes how miserable "Manda" is, stuck in the heat of Florida, having to care for her very ill mother and father as well as Leo, and with a failing marriage to Grant, who loved her when she was young and beautiful but no more... and never having traveled to Paris (she studied French in college). Mina knows the marriage is done for when Grant makes a pass at her and she slugs him.

Mina is the hero of this story. Her mother Sophie— the abandoner, a whore (according to Manda)—was born Caucasian but has turned black with age and become extraordinarily beautiful: "It happens sometimes. No big deal," she says. She sees that Genevieve, Manda's best friend, would sleep with Grant, but only by a chance interruption, doesn't. Mina says these adults are not living and they don't even see it. She decides to drop out of school and live in Paris, the city of light and love (where, if you recall—and I am sure Groff does— Mrs. Ramsay wanted Cam to go because she loved Mr. Ramsay and couldn't leave him to go there herself).

What appalled me was that Grant didn't have the courage to tell his wife he was leaving her—for good—and had to make up an excuse that he was going to a university in the north for better opportunities; not to escape the Florida heat and being enmeshed in his wife's caretaking role without any fun or sex. And that Grant asked Manfred, Genevieve's 30-year older husband—a rich bon vivant of minor royalty with castles and property, now bankrupt because of episodes of manic spending due to his un-medicated bipolar disorder—to cover for him. The sly old fox asks, who is the woman for whom he's leaving his wife and son?

(Ch. 7:) What excited and frightened me was the bold, in-your face eroticism of Helena on vacation in Salvador, Brazil. In her early 30s, sexy and beautiful, she takes care of herself (clothes, makeup) and seeks men, older and younger, businessmen and bellhops, in bars and restaurants, and even takes up with a dangerous, lascivious shopkeeper who rescues her from a violent storm (a projection unto nature of her passions). Although she knows he is a bad man—she has seen him hit a short woman who may be his wife, and has been warned by the owner of the apartment she is renting to shop elsewhere, at a well-lit and cheaper market a few blocks away—Helena repeatedly shops in his bodega to taunt him (unconsciously, perhaps) to abuse her. There is a serious squall; heavy rain and wind bursts while she is in the bodega, preventing her from going home only a few yards away. (Surely she wasn't going to drown, but the storm is meant to inform us of her passion for danger. If this were a movie, the sound track would heighten the suspense.) In the semi-dark, he is trying to get her drunk and rape her (she keeps a cold bottle of beer he has given her as a weapon), but he doesn't because he falls asleep, drunk. But before he sleeps, he sadistically spreads with his dirty fingers a deep gash in her leg she sustained in a fall: the rape.

This frightened me, and I wanted to look away, not read on; but I did. Helena escapes in the morning light but not before she is tempted to care for a wound her rapist has endured during the dark night in the store. She is aware of her dual nature, that she can't escape but can resist; and she leaves without tending him. She writes to her sisters, "stuck in their safe marriages," and a scrubbed version of her adventures to her Catholic mother who attends Mass and worries about her.

It saddened me that these characters did not and could not see the pleasures in riding on a carousel with their children, ask them what treats they really liked, take pleasure in their growing up, value the comfort and loyalty of a partner into old age, and realize that while physical love may abate, dreams of young love, and memories of young love, can last forever-—as long as we believe there is a tomorrow.

Ch. 8: Flower Hunter

Flower Hunters is a translation of a Seminole Indian name *Puc-Puggy*, given to a naturalist, William Bartram.[21] *She* (again, the impersonal character we have met before, with her two unnamed sons and unnamed husband) has been told a week ago—kindly yet firmly—by Meg, her best and only friend, that Meg needs a break from their friendship. That means their sons can't play together; *she* has only an easy-going Labradoodle dog to talk to (we learn soon enough that the dog needs a break too), and

---

[21] *Bartram's Travels* is the short title of naturalist William Bartram's book describing his travels in the American South and encounters with Native Americans between 1773 and 1777. It was published in Philadelphia, Pennsylvania in 1791 by the firm of James & Johnson.

her 16-year marriage has "blurred at the edge of each other's vision." She has fallen in love with a book about the dead naturalist Bartram, whose earthy, exploratory nature has turned on her erotic world of body smells, especially of nursing at the breast and merger of a mother and child, which she realizes is what she wants from Meg and her husband.

She has forgotten it is Halloween and to make or even buy costumes and jack-o'-lanterns for her children, depending on her husband to pick up the slack; he gladly takes them trick-or-treating, wearing an old Mohawk wig himself. She has forgotten the kindergarten's Spooky Breakfast as well, arriving at school with an un-costumed little boy and no "boo-berry" muffins. She is a sour person; she resents giving out candy at the door to the neighborhood kids, preferring to give out toothbrushes. She doesn't enjoy little girls who want to dress as princesses. Bitterly, she thinks, "Meg loves this shit."

"Meg is the best person she knows, far better than herself or her husband, maybe even better than William Bertram....

"Well, William Bartram won't need a break from her. The dead need nothing from us; the living take and take."

What does she want/need to take from Bartram, Meg or her husband? She is no longer afraid of snakes, but fears climate change, small sinkholes becoming bottomless sinkholes from which you can't escape (surely a metaphor for her chronic depression); she fears that "maybe she has become so cloudy to her husband he has begun to look right through her; she's frightened of what he sees on the other side."

But she is unafraid of Bartram, his two sides, the "feeling body and the remembering brain," as shown in his description of a bull gator:

> *"Behold him rushing forth from the flags and reeds. His enormous body swells. His plaited tail brandished high, flouts upon the lake. The waters like a cataract descend from his opening jaws. Clouds of smoke issue from his dilated nostrils. The earth trembles with his thunder."* (Groff's italics.)

This represents masculine power, phallic power over the princess who longs to be protected, who fears and envies it at the same time because it threatens her femaleness, as expressed in Meg: baker, seamstress, and...

> "medical director of the abortion clinic in town... all day has to hold her patients' stories and their bodies, as well as the tragic lack of imagination from the chanting protestors on the sidewalk.... It would be too much for anyone, but it is not too much for Meg."

But she, it appears, wants too much from Meg...to "ride nestled cozily" on her back, as *her* children do. And so, she drives Meg away.

As I read, once again in despair, I resort to the defensive position of the listening, empathic analyst, because I feel helpless in the face of her needs: for sensuality, erotic mother-child, suckling bonding, merging is a better word; and the willingness of Bartram to see in nature, his nature: *"How fantastical looks the libertine Clitoria, mantling the shrubs, on the vistas skirting the groves!"*

The chapter ends with her fantasy of being at the

bottom of a deep sinkhole, "so far down that nobody could get her out, they could only visit... From down there, everyone would seem so happy." She calls her husband and as the phone rings and rings rehearses what she will say—"Babe, I think we have a problem"—she says to the dog, who is looking up at her, "Well, nobody can say that I'm not trying."

Ch. 9: Above and Below

How fast we can fall from the university and from a boyfriend, a teaching fellowship, books and students, to not teaching, no boyfriend, no books, an old car you can't afford to fix or buy gas for, no prospect for another academic job because you made bad choices and didn't take the risk to publish (knowing you would perish if you didn't), living out of your car or on the beach under a tarp (until the car is gutted, trashed, pissed on, left as derelict as you are and without your well-worn copy of *Middlemarch* to keep you company, near starvation, scrounging in grocery store dumpsters for edible unsold food...or wading in a fountain where people throw pennies, feeling ashamed for stealing "someone else's wishes," sweaty and stinking in the Florida heat until you can sneak into a shower room of a fancy beachfront condo and use the soap, shampoo, and razors provided gratis for them?

So starts this story of a fall. Spoiler alert: it gets worse before it gets better...and doesn't end well. What complex circumstances in the lives of these nameless people (for sure, intended to remind us it could be us) is the hook that draws us in or repels us to put the book down.

Curiously, I'm thinking as I write, how *it is human*

nature to name ourselves when we meet strangers; tell them who we are, what we do. One of the most famous first sentences in literature is "Call me Ishmael," and only later, once drawn into the book, wanting to know who he is and why should we care, do we learn that he is the narrator of the story, the only surviving crewmember of the Pequod, the ship destroyed by the great white whale.

As Groff tells us, the hero is a young woman who teaches literature and writing. She is now barely surviving financially, living hand to mouth, but obviously she (the author, as opposed to *she*, the young teacher in the story), both knowing Ishmael and that we want to know her name, refuses to tell us. In the previous story, we know Meg but not *her*. (A writing professor once suggested I read a story, "Bartleby, the Scrivener" by Herman Melville, also the author of Moby-Dick.) Perhaps people who have no better means of adapting to what they feel powerless to change resort to passive resistance?

She, we learn, lost her father when she was ten years old and her mother, out of loneliness, made a bad marriage that her daughter would not accept. The mother lapsed into hypochondriasis, morbid depression and disinterest in her daughter, forgetting her birthday and never reaching out to her when *she* passively retaliated by making desultory, checking-in calls on holidays but never visiting...a stalemate that *she* acted out in her professional life by withholding what her career demanded of *her*.

The power in this story is in *her* life force; unlike in the previous story where she sinks into the sinkhole so deeply that people above can only peer down at her, and life exists beyond her reach. Where does her life force come from? Is it from her DNA, transmitted by her father and his influence in the ten years before he died; from her absorption in books like *Middlemarch* (books are so often the refuge of unhappy children and adults), or from influential teachers or grandparents we don't know about? The text of all of the stories in *Florida* emphasize parental sadism, neglect and abandonment, as well as the accidental good fortune of rescuers, nurturing caretakers, women of heft who hug and snuggle—and later in this story, a lonely janitor gives *her* a job as his helper so she can eat and not have to beg. She becomes his caretaker when he soils himself and becomes the diaper-changing, bathing mother. But he, too, disappears: another abandoner. Shocking reversals and doubling are found in all the stories and so it continues in this story, which alone is worth the price of the book.

What about the ending? (Which I will not give away...except to say it is unexpected, mysterious and is a coded commentary on the title.)

Ch. 10: Snake Stories

Not again. My impulse is to skip this penultimate story. I never wanted to read about snakes again, but I am hooked. I have to trust the author and her editors, who don't want to bore the audience. I read it and I wasn't bored.

It isn't really about snakes, such as those found all over Florida as the narrator mentions, lying in wait to bite and inject us with poison. It's about men; even the best men, *her* good man, her husband, who flirts too closely at parties with a married woman, Olivia. Then there is a divorce; and we don't know yet if *her* husband has divorced her and married Olivia, or if Olivia has been divorced by her husband Omar, or has divorced him. We are told later that Olivia found a snake in her toilet at home—an omen: something was up in *her* marriage that *she* didn't want to look at any more than Olivia wanted to look at the swimming serpent.

The nameless heroine is big on omens. She is at a duck pond with her dog, thinking about how the planet is being raped by men, when she sees a great blue heron whip its head and snare a water snake. "We watched, transfixed, as the bird cracked its head down so hard three times that the snake separated in half, spilling blood. And the heron swallowed one half, which was still so alive that I could see it thrashing down that long and elegant throat." This reminds her of the *Iliad*:

> "For a bird had come upon [the Greeks], as they were eager to cross over, an eagle of lofty flight, skirting the host on the left, and in its talons it bore a blood-red monstrous snake, still alive as if struggling, nor was it yet forgetful of combat, it writhed backward and smote him that held it on the breast beside the neck, till the eagle, stung with pain, cast it from him to the ground and let it fall on the ground in the midst of the throng, and himself with a loud cry sped away down the blasts of the wind.

> "This was an omen, clear and bright. The Greeks did not heed it, and they suffered."

She, a good feminist, complains to her husband (who, as it turns out, has not divorced her) that Eve "gets pegged with all of human sin." And then one day, while walking alone at night on a little-used path, aware of the danger of doing so, she nearly trips over a beautiful girl, bleeding down her thighs, who has been beaten and raped, but who rejects her help—"No fucking cops. No ambulance." The young woman does allow *her* to take her to her home and wash her wounds, but will not accept tea or food. "Fuck off, lady." She then insists she be taken to her own home, a cabin with broken windows and rotting garbage on the front porch. *She* does, however, inform the police and brings them the bloody towels (to be used as DNA evidence to identify the rapist, who, as the victim must know, will kill her next time if he has a chance). A policeman counsels *her* that "you can't help someone if they don't want your help."

We learn that before her marriage, *she* was date-raped in the shower by a "good guy"—a socialist who cried at the movies—but got back into bed with him anyway, and was dumped by him two weeks later. (A #MeToo event.) On New Year's morning, *she* asks her husband, "You think there are still good people in the world?" (We know she has doubted his intentions toward Olivia.) She has never told her good guy, her strong and protective husband, about the rape. But she asks him, are there any good people left? "Oh yes, he said. Billions. It's just that the bad ones make so much more noise."

Ch. 11: Yport

To this tiny French town of Yport, near Calais and Honfleur—two much prettier towns much visited by American tourists like my wife and me—comes the mother along with her two boys, seven and four years of age.

More than 40 years ago, after visiting Utah Beach (pristine and hard to imagine the thousands of lives lost there against machine gunfire, mortars and land mines), and then Pointe du Hoc, where U.S. Army Rangers scaled the 100-foot cliff and walked into the fortified, concrete bunkers manned by Polish POW's with Wehrmacht troops at their backs who would kill them if they tried to desert (stepping into craters as large as golf course sand traps from the day-long bombardment by battleships that never actually penetrated those reinforced concrete bunkers)—my wife and I went to the Memorial Museum and then the American Cemetery, where I sought the graves of young Jewish boys, braver than me, who had family in those camps that it would take two years to liberate. I cried and would have left stones on their graves had it been permitted.

We had come on a pilgrimage to honor the allied dead who fought to liberate Europe, while *she* comes to Yport to escape the Florida heat she hates; to expose her boys to the French language and culture she nostalgically imagines still exists; and to immunize her sons against all that she hates about America: overweight people who have lost whatever moral compass they once had; who are determined to rape the environment so that virgin forests and coral reefs would no longer exist for fish, animals and humans to enjoy, play and procreate in. But she cannot banish her obsessive worries about the survival of mankind, the world she was raising her children to live in. She believes their childhood is the last childhood and she is unable to protect them or anyone from the horrors of being merely imperfect humans. And she only succeeds in frightening them. They want to play and swim, and they know mommy can't join them because she worries about everything.

She has said in the previous story that there are omens to confirm her fears: snakes appear in toilets, predicting infidelity; herons smash snakes and swallow them, writhing, bloody and still alive; she recalls the *Iliad* where an eagle swoops over a Trojan War battlefield and is killed by the monstrous snake in its beak, an omen the Greeks do not heed; men rape and kill with impunity; mothers are cruel to their children. There are more good men than bad men by far, but the bad men get all the attention, or so says her husband; and a kind, gentle man commits suicide after a late-in-life marriage.

Yet, *she*, the mother, is blind to the cruelty she imposes on her boys and her husband. Her little boy misses his father, who is back home in Florida working 18-hour days (we are not told why), but she makes no effort to have the Wi-Fi in their rental cottage fixed because she doesn't like the smelly rental agent who stops by more than once to ask if everything is OK. When she calls her husband by phone (very expensive) instead of Skype, he isn't in and, spitefully, she won't try harder to reach him (because she still isn't sure he didn't want to be unfaithful with Olivia, the married woman he flirted with). The result: the littlest boy thinks Daddy doesn't love him. *She*, determined to only tell the truth, is stumped when her son asks, "Then maybe he doesn't love you?" She doesn't get it. Her son needs a lie to feel secure and she can't give it to him. (Can there be any doubt that Groff has absorbed Virginia Woolf and written an homage to her?)

The ostensible reason *she* has come to Yport, where Americans never vacation, and has disrupted her sons' summer camp vacations—which they miss—is to pursue her literary interest in Guy de Maupassant in the town where he was raised, on the basis of one short story she loves and her kind-of crush on him, with his youthful zest for life and women. But she has avoided writing anything about him for ten years and continues to avoid writing during the few days she spends in Paris and the entire ten days in Normandy; because he (Guy) was a morally corrupt sadist, an anti-Semite and a promiscuous bisexual bully who participated in a violent anal rape of an effeminate man who either bled to death or committed suicide. Guy and his brother, she learns, both died insane as a result of tertiary syphilis. She now says she hates him and tells her children so. They naturally say, *Why did you bring us here? We hate him too, hate it here and want to go home.*

All she wants is for her boys to be good men, independent and able to stand on their own...to know the limits of teasing and quarreling and be able to show affection for each other. The younger boy is outgoing and clearly very smart; his older brother is moody and anxious, but each in their own way can have fun, play, eat ice cream with intense pleasure and enjoy being messy and stinky, as boys are wont to do. They know she loves them deeply and she shows it by letting them *snuggle* (my emphasis of this word we have read before) against her warm body when they are freezing cold and allowing them to swim and play in the sea. (How else do you develop confidence in yourself in life, which, like the sea, can be cold and challenging?)

They know and tell her that she worries too much about everything. And they know that she is depressed, has a serious drinking problem and is worried about the world but not enough about herself.

As the story and book come to a close, she and they know they belong in stinky, humid, alligator- and snake-ridden Florida with their friends and father.

In the end, Lauren Groff is optimistic that if only people can find the good in themselves and others, there is hope for the planet and our imperfect species. But she "isn't promising us a rose garden."

ABOUT THE AUTHOR

HOWARD L. SCHWARTZ, M.D., was born in Bronx, NY in 1937 and raised in Newark, NJ. After graduating from Columbia, Class of '59, he attended what was then the Seton Hall College of Medicine and Dentistry, now Rutgers Medical School. He interned and completed his psychiatric residency at Montefiore Hospital in the Bronx, not far from where he was born. During the Vietnam War, he served as a Lt. Commander in the USNR at the Philadelphia Naval Hospital from 1967–1969. His duties there as head of an admissions unit exposed him to the horrors of war (and to its resulting posttraumatic stress, about which he did not become aware until many years later). Returning to New Jersey to pursue psychoanalytic training at the Downstate Division of Psychoanalytic Education, he became a faculty member there for the next 25 years. As a member of the New Jersey Psychoanalytic Society, he presented and discussed papers and served as President for four years, all the while engaged in full-time psychoanalytic practice.

Always an avid reader, Dr. Schwartz turned to writing his memoirs, stories for his five grandchildren, and two books published by IPBooks: Hide and Seek/Hidden and Found (2017) and All Aboard (2018). The stimulus to write Women: Biology, Culture and Literature evolved from the #MeToo movement. He credits his education at Columbia—especially its "Core Curriculum" and the opportunity to double-minor in Political Science and "Oriental Humanities"— with his continued interest in reading his bucket list of classics and modern literary fiction in what he calls his "permanent semi-retirement."

Balancing Dr. Schwartz's professional life is his marriage of 58 years to a woman who keeps reminding him he sits too much, is his night driver and is largely responsible for their active social life. Spending time with his three children and five grandchildren, hobbies, deep friendships, the rich cultural life of New York City and last but not least yearly vacations in Mexico provide the ballast for his perhaps overactive semi-retirement.

www.ingramcontent.com/pod-product-compliance
Lightning Source LLC
Chambersburg PA
CBHW071236020426
42333CB00015B/1494